THE DEATH OF
DODGE BALL

"THE BEGINNING OF THE END TO AMERICA'S GREATNESS"

BOBBY HERODES

authorHOUSE®

AuthorHouse™
1663 Liberty Drive
Bloomington, IN 47403
www.authorhouse.com
Phone: 1 (800) 839-8640

Published by AuthorHouse   03/28/2019

ISBN: 978-1-7283-0630-8 (sc)
ISBN: 978-1-7283-0629-2 (e)

Library of Congress Control Number: 2019903700

Print information available on the last page.

This book is printed on acid-free paper.

INTRODUCTION

The Death of Dodgeball provides an in-depth look at how parents of my generation have forced their views onto our public education system. These extreme views are single-handedly destroying the most popular game ever created: dodgeball. Over the past thirty years, as a gym teacher in New York State, I have watched, as well as fought against, this assault on our children's journey through their wonder years. Come take a look at our current education system, and reflect on your childhood. What you find might surprise you.

I wrote this book more than ten years ago with the thought that if I kept fighting, I might create a teaching environment that parents and administrators would come to see as essential for our kids. I created Funball. But as my thirty-year teaching and coaching career comes to an end, I've realized that I need help from my fellow Americans. Here is my story.

CONTENTS

CHAPTER 1

The State of the Union

How did we get here? What has led us to the brink of total disaster? How can it be that so many of us have allowed this to happen? With endless checks and balances in our government, culture, and society, we still are all standing by and watching this phenomenon continue on its cruel path. We are tying ourselves to trees in the forests on the West Coast to help save the spotted owl. Many of our beaches on the East Coast are now off-limits so that the little bird called the piping plover might survive into the future. Those same people are helping to speed up the inevitable end of the greatest childhood game ever played: dodgeball.

I am not a smart man; I do not have the ability to assemble children's toys or put together a gas grill from the Home Depot. But I do possess the wisdom to realize when a child's heart is being broken. I can look into the mind and soul of a teenager who needs some time away from the extreme stress that our society has placed on him or her. I and a few other gym teachers around the country have been fighting this battle for almost two decades, and with time running out, I feel compelled to put this on paper for everyone who remembers being a child or has children of his or her own.

Let me say it again. I am a gym teacher; I work in a gym, and there, I teach the many games that kids love to play. My students become physically educated while having fun playing all the games that they need when they are young. I don't feel threatened by the academic world. I don't need a title to be good at what I do. People who think of me as just a gym teacher don't offend me. More often than not, those people are jealous of what I get to do every day at work. A wise man once said, "Find out what you love to do, do it every day, and you will never work a day in your life."

I do get upset at the direction my profession is going, with its emphasis on skill-based curriculum, cooperative games, and activities and movement. These are all wonderful, but they are missing one important thing. Where the hell is the fun in that picture?

Now, for those of you in my profession who feel your blood pressure quickly rising and might soon explode, please step back, relax, and take a nice, long, deep breath. I don't have a problem with you calling yourself a physical education teacher or even a teacher of kinesiology, biomechanics, or movement science. That's great, if that is what you feel is right. Just please stop freaking out when I use the words *gym teacher* at a teachers' conference. What you call yourself doesn't bother me at all, so please extend me the same courtesy.

Dodgeball is on the brink of extinction, if, in fact, it is not already gone for good. Dodgeball isn't just a childhood game. Those of us who have worked with kids know that this game provides children with their first opportunity to understand what life is truly about: we are all impermanent beings, and life is rarely—if ever—fair. Some days, we will shine with greatness, and other days will bring us to tears. Many adults are now afraid to talk to their children about these things because they are more concerned with becoming friends with their children than being their most important teachers in this lifetime.

Other than raising my four children—Anton, Aiden, Avery, and Holden—and growing old with my wife of twenty-six years, Jennifer, putting on paper what I have witnessed and continue to see as a New York State gym teacher will be one of my greatest achievements. I failed many of my English classes when I was a child. To this day, I cannot spell. But please don't judge me on my ability to write, as that's not what this is about. My strength is that I can communicate through the spoken word. I have been able to reach out to thousands of kids by talking to them. I am doing this on my own and realize my weaknesses. I don't know where to turn; I don't have the resources to have a ghostwriter help me. And if parts of the story don't make sense, you can call me at the high school where I teach. If I am not teaching a class or having a pick-up game, I will clearly explain those parts to you.

When I began writing this book, I didn't want it to become political in nature, but as time passed, it became very difficult to avoid that. Behind our government, the second-most politicized field of work in our country is education. So in many ways, what dodgeball is going through has varying political aspects to it. But in reality, dodgeball is not a political issue. It is a human issue.

As humans, like any other animals, we are born, are young for a period of time, grow old, and then die. And like many other animals, when we are young, we love to play games. Some of us never grow up and love to play games our entire lifetimes. To play a game that allows you to show true emotion and have freedom of expression, the thrill of competition, and the agony of defeat is priceless.

That is dodgeball.

To be fair, years ago, many gym teachers did take pleasure in seeing others in pain. Many of these gym teachers were never true athletes themselves and harbored a deep-seated anger for never having won the championship when they were players. Often, they blamed their coaches for their lack of success. These gym teachers never took responsibility for their actions and always looked for an excuse when things fell apart. They always looked outward at the world around them when they failed, rather than looking inward to find out what they could have done differently to change the outcome of the big games. They became gym teachers for all the wrong reasons and, as a result, never were able to connect with their students and players. In the end, they lived very sad, lonely existences. They might have attained many awards as coaches that covered the walls of their offices, but those were all they had. Those metal and granite objects froze in time, while the students who actually acquired those prizes tried to forget their selfish, arrogant, and ignorant gym teachers.

I apologize to those thousands of students who never had the opportunity to realize their potential as dodgeballers. But do we throw away a game that created so many memories because of a few bad eggs?

I hope that my words help you take a long, hard look at who you were when you were a child—and who you are in the present. I try to do this daily, but I find it hard as I continue to fight a powerful opponent: "good intentions." I remember my grandfather always saying, "The road to hell was paved with good intentions." If that is true, you can see that I am up against a great competitor. I do believe in my heart that many people think that they are doing the right thing by going to board of education meetings and trying to make playgrounds and gyms safer for their children. Their intentions are good, but they are shortsighted in theory, wisdom, and compassion.

People employ a similar theory every winter in upstate New York. Many well-intentioned people feed the white-tailed deer during the cold and snowy months, not aware of the catastrophic results that will occur next year or the year after. I grew up in a small upstate town called Middleburgh. It is in Schoharie County, about thirty-five minutes west of Albany. Growing up in the country, I was able to hunt, fish, and trap the wildlife that surrounded me every day. Every moment that I wasn't playing sports I spent in the great outdoors.

While rabbit hunting one cold January day, a vision forever burned into my memory. I saw what looked to be a large, healthy white-tailed deer lying in the tall grass near the woods. As I got closer, the deer remained in the same spot, motionless. I continued to walk very slowly until I was less than five feet from the doe. All four of her legs were broken, snapped in half due to malnutrition. I could tell that she had been lying there for a long time. After ending the deer's suffering, I contacted the local environmental conservation officer, who then dissected the deer and found inside the deer's stomach pebbles, small stones, sticks, and anything else that the deer could shove in to try to fight off its hunger.

By the end of that hunting season, I lost count of the dead deer that I came across. The mass die-off was due to the many people who had fed the deer years before, which had allowed the herd to populate far above what the habitat could sustain. The conservation officer went on to say that this cycle would continue until people realized that nature and animals have survived for millions of years without the good intentions of humans, and these people need to understand that nature will take care of itself. If the white-tailed deer cannot adapt to their ever-changing environment, they will one day become extinct no matter what we humans do.

Many school districts across the state of New York have already banned dodgeball, mostly due to parents and their relentless desire to try to save their children from the dangers of being a kid. Intervening in our public schools in this way is exactly the same as how the people tried to help the deer survive through the harsh, cold winter. For sure, those deer made it through one tough year, but what about the future? What is so troubling about this involvement with our public schools is that we may not see the damage until fifteen to twenty-five years down the road, when an entire generation may have many problems in the adult world, all because we, as parents, did not allow our kids to grow up with all the ups and downs that they will go through every day of their lives. This is the main point to my short story that I will try to convey to you.

Going a step further, some school districts in Massachusetts and New Jersey have even banned playing tag at recess and in gym class. Instead, they will hold organized recess time for twenty minutes a day to satisfy the state's requirement for gym class and recreation, while taking away their children's only free time of the day to create, play, and express themselves during recess. If this is allowed to happen, it will rob many students of the very nature of being a child in a social environment. They defend their actions by stating that the schools will pick up another forty-five minutes during the day that they can devote to academics to help their students get ahead of the game, while totally missing the picture that the "games" are all that really matter for these young children. This is just the tip of the iceberg when it comes to the logic that many school districts across the country are employing.

Some parents feel that their children are safer now that they will not be chased around the playground and possibly fall, skinning a knee or an elbow. They may be right, for now, which, problematically, is another thing that our culture is obsessed with: the "now," instant gratification, immediate resolution. That is not life. I call this belief *shortsighted compassion.* They truly believe that what they are doing is in their children's best interest, and while today that may be true, what about their future? Remember, as parents, our job never ends. There is no finish line. There is no end zone. We never get to spike the football after the winning touchdown. We chose to have children, and we will be their parents until we pass away. This means that we must do what is right for them today, tomorrow, and far into the future. More often than not, that means they absolutely need that skinned knee or elbow when they are young so that they have the opportunity to feel physical pain from the wound and emotional pain from losing the game. Then and only then will they have practiced what it is like to live in our society, body and mind.

The Greeks knew that both physical and emotional pain were essential for all human existence. So what about when that young child finally grows up and goes for that first job interview, never having had the opportunity to experience competition, feel the pain of losing the contest, or think on his or her feet, and can't answer the questions with confidence? Will Mom or Dad call the employer and tell them that they didn't take the time to really get to know their young adult? If children never have the opportunity to compete, play, and create with other students without structure, they won't have those skills when they grow up.

Dodgeball was the one activity that gave students the opportunity to step into the real world even as children, but without the consequences of failing as an adult. The consequence of failing in dodgeball was that you were out. You had to go sit on the sideline until someone on your team caught a ball to bring you back in. All that time spent on the sideline gave you time to reflect on why or how you got eliminated and how you could never make that same mistake again. That time sitting out is absolutely essential.

Cooperative games never have that "out time" that is so important to a child's psychological development. Many teachers have students play tagging games where when players get hit, tagged, or captured, the players just have to attempt five jumping jacks, or maybe five sit-ups, and then they can come right back into the game. Yes, the students get cardiovascular exercise, but this doesn't train them psychologically and emotionally. So in these instances, only the body receives the benefit, not the mind. Those teachers are only doing half their job. When students get trapped in a prison, or wait on a line, they cheer, hope, and pray that someone on their team rescues them and gets them back into the game. Here, they develop the concept of survival, family, or teamwork—the idea that we all need someone's help once in a while on this earth. Consequences are critical. Consequences are one of the variables that guide us on our journey. Through them, a child begins to understand the world around him or her. It is a fact that if a child in art class never uses a pair of scissors to cut out a paper project, he or she will never, ever get cut by scissors, but he or she will also not have that wonderful project to bring home to Mom and Dad before open house. If there are no consequences, then he or she is not living.

It is just like having to discipline your own child; when done correctly, it hurts the parent just as much as the child. No parent, teacher, or coach likes disciplining his or her children, but it is your job, so do it! Have the courage and the wisdom to say what needs to be said, do what needs to be done.

That's how the human mind has evolved. If we lose dodgeball, we run the risk of ending human evolution as we know it today. If a child never runs, his or her chances of falling significantly go down. But that child will never know how fast he or she can run. Yes, we may save ourselves from a few bumps and bruises along the way, but the journey is the most exciting part of our existence, not the destination. Once we reach our destination, we smile, stand there for a moment, realize that we can't stay there forever, and then head off on another journey, having no idea where it will lead us.

Believe it or not, the Industrial Revolution has played a huge role in the downfall of dodgeball, and organized premier sports are responsible for much of the pressure that dodgeball has received over the past twenty years. And our higher-education prep schools, colleges, and universities also have to share the blame. Many of the great institutions that our country has been built on are under assault, and we may soon only talk about dodgeball in history textbooks. The parents of this new generation of children are our only hope if we are to preserve this game of dodgeball and, more important, this way of life for many years to come.

Now, don't get me wrong; not everyone loved dodgeball the way that I did when I was a kid. Some children hated dodgeball. Having a red rubber ball thrown at them scared them to death. The difference between those who hated dodgeball and those who lived for the game is simple. I, who loved the game, am not trying to tell people how to best live their lives. Those who hated dodgeball now believe that they know how best to raise your children. They think they know what is right and wrong when it comes to our school districts. The fact is, if they ever took the time to listen to their children, they might gain some important wisdom that they greatly lack: the wisdom to allow their children to try something and stick with it for a period of time, pick them up when they fall down, give them a kick in the ass when they need it, and, when it's over, allow those children to decide whether that thing is for them.

Here, the political similarities rear their ugly heads. Those with a liberal democratic point of view in our government and society believe they know how to best spend your tax dollars. They can invest your money better than you can. They know what foods are good for you far better than you do. So, most cafeterias in our public schools are devoid of cookies because granola is better. All that I want is a damn package of cookies after my lunch; is that too much to ask for? They know for a fact that humans are causing our planet to warm up, yet the planet seemed quite balmy when the dinosaurs owned this real estate long before humans were even a dream. Back then, you could pick up waterfront property dirt cheap. Now, you can't touch anything on the water for under $500,000. They think that the world should be fair and that we should all experience the same things in life. Well, that's not our world, or even our country. Not only did many of these politicians hate dodgeball, they loathed the game. And they have never been able to move on from the fact that life isn't fair.

We all have our own special qualities, and once we have gained enough wisdom to understand what we are good at, we create passion and pursue those dreams. My dreams are not the same as yours, so don't try to force my children into your dreamland, when our kids have many millions of options today. You will never see me in front of a car dealership with a picket sign saying, "SUVs kill," or by a Dunkin' Donuts with a sign that says, "Dunkin' Donuts are poison, they are loaded with trans fats."

What always made our country the greatest in the world is that we were free to live the way we wanted to, without restrictions from those who had views that differed from ours. But across the country, our public schools are under assault from those who hated dodgeball. And if we don't wake up, it will be lost forever.

Before I go any further, I want to remind you that this story comes from one man's point of view, and you are free to agree or disagree with what I say. My observations come from the past thirty-nine years, from the day I threw my very first dodgeball to the present. Now, I may glorify some of my childhood memories, but the memories over the past thirty-nine years come from working with humans of all shapes and sizes, ages, colors, races, and religions. I have taught elementary students for fourteen years and high-school-age students for fifteen years, and I spent one year as a graduate assistant at West Chester University. I have coached four-year-old soccer players up to NCAA Division I athletes. I have taught countless clinics to adults who range in age from twenty-five to sixty-five. So I believe that I can now speak from the standpoint of wisdom.

Maybe you have noticed I have used the word *wisdom* a few times already. I feel the need to expand on what wisdom really means to me. *Wisdom* is defined as "the ability to see the true nature of existence" or, in simplified terms, the ability to see the true nature of a situation, being, or event. This is very hard to put on paper, but I will try. The most common way of gaining wisdom is to live very long and experience many things during life, and never make the same mistake twice. It is very hard to gain wisdom just by growing old, because many of us will make the same mistake about one hundred times before we get it right.

Another way to gain wisdom is to study and practice the true nature of the mind—again, very difficult to do in our current fast-paced society. The third way to gain wisdom is to have it thrust upon you during very traumatic situations at any age. That is how I began to cultivate the limited amount of wisdom that I have drawn on during my time as a teacher and parent.

As an example of the third way to gain wisdom, take a look at any young child who has ever had to deal with the deadly disease of cancer. At a very young age, those children are forced to realize what is truly important in life. They should be playing games and laughing, but they are attached to wires, tubes, and mechanical devices that are sustaining their young lives. Most of these children are peaceful and often have to comfort their parents as they watch them go through their treatment. How can these young children understand what's at stake? They can because they have been forced to see the true nature of their situation, which is wisdom. As I continue with the story, hopefully, you will understand what I mean when I use the term *wisdom*.

When I am forced to talk about the political aspect of dodgeball in this book, I express that most Americans can only identify with one of two distinct points of view: (1) the conservative, right-wing point of view or (2) the liberal, left-wing perspective. If I use the terms *liberal* and *conservative*, I do it to save time. I ask that you step back and look at my situation from the standpoint of wisdom. If more people took the time to actually look at the true nature of what we argue about, it would become very clear that sometimes our intentions are good but they are not based in truth and reality. So please try to be honest with yourself as you read on, because if you're not, you may never gain that ability to see the true nature of this situation, or many other situations that may occur during your lifetime.

Let me explain one more critical aspect of my passion for dodgeball and, in general, this way of life. I do have compassion for the spotted owl out west, and I enjoy watching a bald eagle glide across the sky. But I understand that all living creatures are subject to the law of impermanence, which means that one day, they will die, and one day in the future, if they cannot adapt to the changing environment, they will become extinct. So when I talk to you about dodgeball becoming extinct, I am well aware of the fact that it must also adapt and evolve if it is to survive. Fortunately for me and my students, I noticed its rapid decline about twenty years ago—and I have spent thousands of hours since then working very hard at trying to help dodgeball evolve and adapt to the new, more liberal environment that has taken over our public schools. At the end of the story, I will introduce you to an exciting, amazing game that has evolved out of dodgeball.

But for now, I would like you to take a step back to your childhood and try to remember what you believed to be true about who you were as a person. Over my many years of teaching, I have taken the time to break down all my players into five different player categories. They are the (1) killer, (2) wallflower, (3) jock, (4) brain, and (5) dodger. See if you can find out who you were when you stepped foot into your gym class to play dodgeball, and also who you would be today if you were to get into one of the many adult dodgeball leagues that have popped up around the country. (I find it very interesting that many adults in my generation are getting involved with dodgeball leagues, kickball leagues, wiffle ball leagues, and tournaments around the country. The reason for this development is simple: these games were very exciting and fun when we were kids, and they are just as fun as adults. Please keep this in mind as I continue on with the story.)

Before I talk about one of my special players I love named the *killer*, I need to clarify a few things. Right now, you are reaching for your telephone to call your senator and file a formal complaint against me and my book. Before you pick up the phone, read on for a few more lines, even as your mind races and you can't understand how I could be so irresponsible as to use the term *killer* in the educational realm when so many school shootings happen every single year across our great country. Now remember, I want you to take a look at the true nature of this situation. Try to keep your hypocrisy to a minimum. How can it be that for many years, the mainstream sport of volleyball has used the term *kill*, referring to a point won by a player on the court, but dodgeball has no right to that exclusive word? Am I wrong? Are we to use that word only when it is politically correct? Does anyone own the rights to the word? I have used the term *kill* in dodgeball for my entire career. And if you want to see true joy, watch a child and see how proud he or she looks when he or she eliminates an opponent in the arena of dodgeball. So don't freak out now; you're progressing nicely.

By the way, those many students who have committed horrible shootings in our public schools did so only after many years of suffering. And if our mainstream media continues to cover and glorify these students, you will see many more in the near future. When children are in pain, they want the world around them to recognize them and help them. Some of the students in our public schools who remain in pain today stay glued to the press coverage that continues for many days after these incidents. For many of these students who are suffering, media coverage of their deaths seems good enough for them, and they see this as a way to finally be heard by their peers and loved ones.

As I wrote this portion of the book on November 29, 2007, three teens were arrested at the Arlington School District in Lagrangeville, where my family lives, right here in my backyard, for plotting a Columbine-style massacre for the year 2010, when they would all be seniors. Everyone seems so shocked when it happens in the school district that their children attend. You may not want to hear this, but almost every middle school and high school across the country has a number of students who, in the right circumstances, would attempt to reach out to the world around them in this style. It is just that students are getting smarter and do not communicate what they truly think until they feel secure that the student they are talking to thinks the same way they do.

When a young child feels hopeless and angry, the mind travels to very dangerous places. And once a child's mind has the capability to focus on a topic and the desire to stick with something, it adds the final ingredients to the recipe for disaster. These kids often need distractions during long days at school, and dodgeball provided a great way for these students to run, throw, jump, dodge, smile, and laugh. It may be just enough to help them realize that everything really isn't that bad.

By now, you think that you have me all figured out. This guy is just another right-wing, gun-toting, radical Christian NRA member.

Well, if you must know, I do own a few guns, and I still go hunting and trapping with my children every season. I am not a member of the National Rifle Association, but I do support the constitutional right to bear firearms. Gun control will only affect the law-abiding citizens; criminals will always have their guns no matter what laws are put on the books.

I am a registered Democrat, but my beliefs come from my grandfather's generation, when the Democratic Party was twice as conservative as the Republican Party of today. My grandpa told me that the Democratic Party was the party that believes in family and in strong values. He would always say, "You're a Herodes, and never forget that." He installed pride in the family, and as a result, I have never wavered in my beliefs of what is right and what is wrong. My grandfather passed away when the restructuring of American politics was almost complete. I haven't voted Democrat for nearly twenty years, and I will always take the time to listen to the points of view of all the candidates who are vying for a position.

I was baptized Methodist, but after a religion class when I was nine, the teacher told my mother, who picked me up from church, to never bring me back again. I don't remember what I did to warrant being thrown out of the Methodist school, but it must have been pretty bad.

Prior to my first open-heart surgery, I started to learn how to meditate, and I soon realized that I had been practicing a primitive form of Buddhism for most of my life. After researching, I entered the Kagyu lineage. This lineage of Tibetan Buddhism focuses on meditation as the main avenue to reaching true joy and peace. This lineage has many levels, and I have come to realize that I am an infant when it comes to the wisdom that many have attained. My Buddhist name is Karma Tenpa Gyaltsen, which translates to "victory banner of the teachings." I've always found it interesting that when my Lama named me, he had no idea that I had been a teacher for almost fifteen years.

Now, let's move on and learn about these wonderful kids who are in jeopardy of losing dodgeball if we don't do something quickly.

CHAPTER 2

My Players

The Killer

The killer is a pro. This kid means business each and every time he steps on the floor. He comes to play every day; as a matter of fact, I believe that he spends his spare time honing his skills with rocks, snowballs, and dirt bombs. You can see the killer every day on the playground; in fact, you can't miss him.

Killers walk wherever they go. It's a sign of fear if you move any faster, and believe me, these kids don't have fear, or that is what they want the general public to think. I know the true story. This player has a part-time job by the time he is in fourth grade. Ask a killer to empty his pockets. There is always money in them. It may only be five dollars, but he will always have some. The common person may not consider these legitimately earned wages, but he will always have money.

These players are masters of their emotions; they have been trained by the best. They won't let themselves get too high or too low. Again, these are signs of weaknesses, and God forbid the killer would ever tip his hat. The most you will ever get out of killers is a slight nod; that is exactly what they do when they walk through the gym doors and Coach says, "Kids, we're gonna play dodgeball today." If you're lucky, a slight twinge might come from the corner of their mouth. I know that look—the look that says, "Somebody is gonna go down today." Incidentally, this is just what they would say, if they ever spoke.

These people are angry. They harbor an anger unlike any other anger; this anger comes from these kids' heart. This anger can't control itself, and why should it? It doesn't know its true consequences and what anger can do to a person. Killers haven't lived long enough to know what anger can do. I have seen this anger come in over one hundred different shapes and forms, but it is all the same; it is a child's anger. I have seen it pluck its own eyebrows right out of its head. I have seen it scratch its own skin until it bleeds all over the gym floor. Silent anger hides like a panther in the jungle, always waiting for its next victim to wander into its territory. The killer can sometimes wait hours, days, or even weeks to get his victim.

This player can really hold a grudge. He is the master of his environment when among his peers. He doesn't believe in a world run by democracy. Killers go back a few hundred or even a thousand years, to the days when dictators ruled the world. They choose brute force and power as their management style, with a little intimidation sprinkled in for their own amusement. As far as I can tell, this is how the killer satisfies his need to have the world recognize him.

These players are survivors, and dodgeball is a useful training method of how to obtain excellence in their trade. It has always bothered me that adults feel so threatened by these kids that they immediately form an opinion, put up a wall, and rarely take a moment to search for what makes up these truly special people. (In case I haven't mentioned it yet, all my players are very special people.) It strikes me as strange that the very people who can help these children are the same people who can bring them down. So it goes; the killer is a special person in my mind. He survives despite all the mixed signals he gets from the moment he is born into this world. Let's face it; we all need to be loved, and why should it matter how someone obtains this love, even if it comes at the expense of others?

Long live the killer.

The Wallflower

This player adds a wonderful dimension to my life of dodgeball. The wallflower is a timid, shy mouse who scurries along the back wall of the gym. If wallflowers could, they would disappear into the mortar and bricks that make up the gym walls. The word *dodgeball* strikes fear into the hearts and souls of wallflowers. You can see it in the way that they enter the gym. Their shoulders slump as if they were carrying a hundred law books in their backpack. Their eyes fix to the floor, just hoping and praying that they didn't just hear what they think they heard. They say to themselves, *It's got to be a bad dream. Please, somebody, wake me up.*

The wallflowers don't like any type of confrontation; in fact, I have seen wallflowers pass a killer in the hall and walk so close to the wall that they run into the water fountain. The wallflower will do anything to avoid a conflict. The wallflower is such an interesting person when you get to know him, but that's just the problem; very few people ever do get the chance. No one wants to be seen talking to a wallflower. If you do, they will find you, and as little Billy Brain found out, it could cost you dearly.

Wallflowers are always a little anxious, and as a result, many instances during the school day can cripple one of them with fear, such as lunch. It's possible that nothing causes these children more anxiety than dropping a lunch tray in the cafeteria. It begins when that square tray starts to slide from their fingertips. One corner dips toward the floor; they react by trying to adjust their grip with their other hand. At the same time, their knees start to buckle, feet sliding to get closer to the unbalanced object. The hair on the back of their neck starts to itch; a cold sweat immediately breaks out and covers their entire body. Just when they believe they have avoided a catastrophe, the tray tumbles and catches the corner of their knee and releases all of its contents on their leg and the pseudo-tile floor in the cafeteria. They think, *It's over; my life is over, all because I felt sorry for that stupid wallflower out at recess.* All it takes is a little bump from a jock on his way to the table, and the tray hits the floor with a resounding sound that only hardened plastic can make. Lesson learned. *Don't feel sorry for anyone anymore at any time*; this is what children learn at a young age.

Ironically, when killers drops a tray, that same incident that can bring wallflowers or other children to their knees seems to magically raise up the killers and place them on a pedestal. As the killer's tray hits the floor with that clang of plastic, the killer immediately leans back, raises his arms high and wide, and holds out a double peace sign to his roaring disciples, as Richard Nixon did just before boarding his aircraft after resigning. That same loud roar erupting from the cafeteria that can paralyze the wallflower suddenly turns into a roar of celebration, of victory, signaling the great achievement of a child in an adult-run world. The killer knows that he is in big trouble, the students know that he is in big trouble, yet they celebrate their small victory against the establishment together. At the end of the day, students pass by the detention center, offering support, praise, and general good wishes to the killer as he does his time for trying to embarrass the system. But as the day comes to an end and the school empties, life starts to return to normal. As the next sunrise comes over the hill, it will bring order back to their young lives, and as the first bell rings, everyone will settle into their classroom seats.

This is what makes childhood so wonderful and special; young minds are not yet able to categorize memory as their counterparts, the adults, do. Come to think of it, this may be how many of my players survive these wonder years—selective memory. They push deep inside all those painful encounters that they don't want to remember. The wallflowers are the true masters of this skill, and why not? They get thousands of opportunities to practice this skill each and every day.

How do these players become the wallflowers? The adults all have their theories and spend countless hours in meetings trying to figure out what makes the wallflowers tick. If they want to crack the big secret and find out what they are about, why not try something revolutionary and talk with the wallflowers, not to each other? These adults race from one crisis to the next, trying to find the quick fix, searching to solve all the world's problems, when maybe they should let the kids be kids for more than a few years. Maybe, just maybe, the wallflower doesn't need to be fixed; he may just need some companionship during his daily life. After all, we are social animals, and all animals need to be accepted by the clan, or else they will soon wander off into the great abyss.

Wallflowers are who they are because of their genetics. Do me a favor: the next time you see a wallflower dropped off at school, take a quick peek into his or her parent's minivan, and tell me what you see. Yes, it is what you think—a bigger, older, grayer wallflower. In my eyes, the wallflowers are truly wonderful people, and without them, this world wouldn't be so special.

The Jock

The jock is the one player who truly lives and breathes every day to compete. It is in his blood. The jock has to be the first person in line every time. It doesn't matter what he does in life. Whatever it is, he must immediately turn it into a competition. These players are blessed with not only athletic ability but the psychopathic drive to take this ability to the next level.

Jocks never squeeze the ball too tight; the grip is always just right, tight, spiraling throws that hit the target nearly 95 percent of the time. These kids can play. Rules—the rules are everything to the jocks. The jocks rarely cheat; that's how they view their world. As a matter of fact, not only do most jocks perform at a high level, but while they are performing, they can referee at the same time. And, boy, they will let you know when you are out. They will scream, "Hey, Sammy Wallflower, *you're out*!" at the top of their lungs.

The jocks obsess over the rules to the point that it sometimes becomes their demise. I have seen a jock work himself into a frenzy over the rules of the game. And before you know it, the jock loses focus, turns his head, and bends down to pick up a ball, never noticing the killer standing three feet away with a cocked arm ready to release a lethal blow to the jock. *Bam!* A direct hit to the left shoulder. He looks up with disbelief so real, taking a quick look over at the gym teacher;

a subtle nod, and the jock is gone. But when push comes to shove, the jock is the most polished player in the game.

Another character flaw that the jock has is that he thinks he is never wrong. Many a jock has been led into the principal's office for that reason alone. For one reason or another, this seems built into jocks' makeup; they can't admit it. I have often wondered what it must be like to always be fighting inside oneself. This has got to wear down even the strongest jock both physically and mentally. Where does it come from? If my theory stands the test of time, it will undoubtedly point to the jock's birth parents. One could wonder what might happen if a jock were born from wallflower parents. Could it happen? What would be the result? Would this result in a gross mutation of a person? Or maybe a more well-adjusted young person? Think about it for a minute—a highly skilled athlete with the quiet manners of a wallflower. I think that we may be on to something.

The jocks always change for gym class. They rarely play in their jeans because they know that it might slow them down. They like to make sure that all the variables are stacked in their favor, as opposed to the killers. The killers never changes for gym class. Why bother? It's only gym class. Many a time, I have had a jock enter the gym with a note from his parents asking if he could sit out for class that day due to an injury that occurred the night before in a soccer game. The intelligent jocks will usually wait until I have announced what we will be doing in class that day before they hand me the note. If we are playing dodgeball, they just crumple up the note and throw it into the trash. The more unorganized jock will hand me the note as soon as he comes into the gym. I usually ask how the game went, if they won or lost, and how the injury occurred. Then I will let him know that we are playing dodgeball for the day, and the response is always the same: "Well, maybe I could just give it a try and see how it feels after I warm up."

I love the jock. I just smile and say, "Just go slow; you don't want to injure it any more." Either way that you look at it, the jocks are the finest players in this game, and even if they do have their little quirks, without them, the game would go on forever like the dull taste of chewing gum. Make friends with a jock; you never know when you might need his expertise.

The Brain

As I start to write about the brain, I begin to become self-conscious for fear of messing up my grammar. The brain should be self-explanatory, but it is far from that. He seems to always have a subtle smirk on his face when he walks into the gym. Never cocky, just smirky. As far as his playing ability goes, the brain gets it done most of the time. He doesn't have the jock's athletic ability, but you see, often he doesn't need it. The brain has the exact coordinates of the gym floor memorized. He knows the square footage, the height of the basketball rims, and every piece of floor tape across the gym floor. All these pieces of information are kept stored, locked away for easy access at all times. He knows which jocks are right-handed and those who use their left hands to do their damage. He can give you a psychological profile on every killer in the school, and you know what? He's on the money most of the time.

The brain leaves nothing to chance. He takes all the variables of the game of dodgeball into consideration before the first whistle blows. Strategy—this is the brain's survival technique. The brain always attacks the wallflower first, and then, he will go for the dodger. After seeing success with those two groups, he is forced to choose between the jock and the killer. He will next go for the killer. At this point, the brain is in over his head athletically, but remember, many wars were won in the planning.

The planning that the brain puts into his game often amazes me. I marvel at the way he communicates during the game. At the first sign of a jock getting upset that an opponent is cheating, the brain goes in for the kill. "Hey, Kenny Jock, it sure did look like you got that wallflower out, but it seems like they disagree with your call." Before long, the jock will lose his cool and possibly say something that only Coach can say. This may force Coach to render a decision as to whether the profanity was bad enough to elicit suspension from the game. And depending on

Coach's mood, nine out of ten times, the penalty will be a one-game suspension, a true dagger into the jock's heart. Remember, the jock lives for the game, and the worst possible thing that can happen to a jock is to be forced to sit and watch. Amazing—truly amazing.

The brain has his problems as well. Similar to the wallflower, he doesn't spend time with too many friends during the school day. You see, to be a brain's friend, you often have to agree with the brain's hypothesis on the evolution of man or the molecular structure of argon gas. Children like to be heard, so it is very hard for them to listen to adults all day and in their free time be forced to listen to a child. For this reason, brains sometimes struggle through the school day. But they will be okay. They always are.

The brain also has the ability to dream wonderful dreams, and when you're a kid, dreaming is 99 percent of the game of life. As I said at the beginning of the chapter, my players are very special, and the brains are no exception. They balance out the floor at game time.

The Dodger

The dodger is my final player I would like to tell you a bit about. These kids are the conservationists of the game. Greenpeace comes to mind when I think about the dodgers. They are always looking out for the small guy, the guy who never gets treated nicely at recess. The dodgers have a heart of gold and often wear it right on their sleeve. They don't like what's going on with the earth today. They talk about the ozone layer at the North and South Poles. They admittedly are against the fur trade in modern society. They say, "Hey, it's the year 2018; why the hell do you need to wear muskrats around your neck to keep warm in the winter? Haven't you heard about Gore-Tex?" These kids honestly believe that they can make a difference in the world today, just by what they say and do. They are the true idealists.

Some dodgers are very good athletes, but they disagree with the violence involved with sports today. They will always ride a bike instead of taking a cab if they can. Just by doing that little deed, they feel good that they may have extended the life span of our earth. They are great at debating. That part in the movie *Old School* when Will Ferrell represents the fraternity in the debate challenge always comes to mind when I think about the dodger. And above all, the dodger has more passion pound for pound than any other of my players in the game. I respect the passion that dodgers have for their views, even if they are still too young to sometimes see the true nature of every situation.

Let me tell you something; they are fun to watch. Rarely does the dodger ever pick up the ball. You see, the dodgers inflict their pain by moving swiftly around the court and forcing the jock and killer to be on their best game if they are to get the dodgers out. The dodgers refuse to throw the ball at an opponent; they just wait for the right moment and take the opponent out by catching the ball as he throws it at them. In dodgeball, if you catch the opponent's ball before it hits the ground, the thrower is out. And this is exactly what the dodger plans to do.

Many dodgers are misunderstood. They can't understand why everyone else doesn't agree with them on the issues that face our world today. Stop a dodger in the hall, and ask him about global warming. For the next hour, you will hear a thought-out, well-spoken thesis on why it is happening, how it is happening, and what you can do to stop its inevitable destruction of the earth as we know it. They are always well informed—in my opinion, maybe too well informed. To worry, truly worry, about these types of thoughts as a child is somewhat disturbing. I ask myself, *Where do these dodgers come from? Why are they talking about their cholesterol level as third graders? How come their snack is always carrot sticks and never Oreos? Do the dodgers learn these ideas from the world around them as they grow? Or are they spoon-fed by someone else—maybe an older dodger?*

I'm not one to point fingers. Many times, as I would walk out of the cafeteria with my tray of food—one chocolate milk, one white milk, and a pack of Linden's chocolate-chip cookies—I would hear a second grader saying, "Mr. Herodes, how come every day you buy a pack of cookies? You know you are going to have high cholesterol." Now, tell me how in the hell do seven-year-olds even know how to pronounce *cholesterol?* Don't they deserve even a few years of worry-free existence before the mainstream media worries them into an early grave?

Many nights, at our dinner table, I will have a small TV on in the corner of the room to catch some of the day's news, and my son Aiden has said before, "Dad, please turn off the news. I can't listen to it any more." He is only ten years old. And yes, I know I shouldn't have the TV on during the family dinner, but there are only so many hours in the day to stay in touch with the world around you.

Well, I can only tell you what I see and hear, and again, the dodger is a wonderful person with so much to give to the world, and he rounds out the game that I love—dodgeball. Now that you have met my players, you may find that you were a combination of two or more of them. I hope that I have brought some of those childhood memories back to you today. If some of those memories are sad and painful, I can only apologize again for the gym teachers of your wonder years. Those of you who are feeling that pain again, I plead with you to read on. I will try to explain why and how dodgeball is on the verge of extinction, and maybe you will be able to manage your pain as you take a look at dodgeball from a different perspective. And those of you who now have a big smile on your face after reading about my players, I also need you to understand one thing: that you have a voice in our great nation. And many young children are counting on you to get involved in a different way than you are used to. You will have to modify your involvement so that you can help cultivate an environment that will challenge our children, not coddle them or organize or plan their days for them.

I know how busy you are. Remember, I have four children, now twenty-four, twenty-two, nineteen, and seventeen years old. I know that you are very involved in your child's day. I remember racing home to grab half a peanut butter and jelly sandwich at 5:30 to get child number 1 to soccer practice and circling around to pick up number 3 from ballet. Then, I would race back home to watch my wife get dinner started before religion started at 7:15. This remains but an average day for my wife, my mother-in-law, and me whenever I am not coaching after school. If we all were to stop, sit down, and really look at what we do, we might go insane.

This is not the type of involvement that I am talking about; it is completely different from that. For example, when your child comes up to you on a Sunday morning and says he or she is bored and wants to do something, your involvement and response is simple: "You should go find something to create for yourself that won't put you in jeopardy of losing an arm or a leg." So many of my generation of parents are deathly afraid that their children will grow up hating them. I find it hard to understand this thinking. Twenty to thirty years ago, boredom was one of the most important times in my life. I didn't like being bored, but it forced me into thinking beyond my normal thoughts. It pushed me into creating games to play with my sisters. Yes, of course, it also led me into trouble at times, but I made it through in the end.

I would go as far as to say that because our children are so programmed that they don't have any time to be bored, it is affecting their ability to be creative. From the time they wake up to the time they go to bed, we are shuttling them all across our great nation. And I really mean *nation*. You'll see what I mean when I get to the part of the book that talks about premier sports. Many ten- and eleven-year-old athletes compete not only in their hometowns but in the next state over, and if their team is very proficient, it may even travel halfway across the country to compete in the many national tournaments that are held every year in many premier sports. But for now, let's just talk about how our involvement must change, or else our children will suffer in the future.

CHAPTER 3

Superstar

Believe it or not, this involvement was born after the Industrial Revolution. Now, I know that you think that I have completely gone off the deep end. Up until the period in our country called the *Industrial Revolution*, our families worked all the time to survive. This was just a fact of life here and in other nations around the world. Before we had machines and computers to help make our work easier, we did everything manually. But after the Industrial Revolution, adults' leisure time slowly started to increase. This leisure time ties directly into one of the major factors that has pushed dodgeball and other unorganized games closer to extinction. Let me explain.

Thirty years ago, very few areas in our country had premier sports, other than Little League baseball. Very few towns had organized sports, such as soccer, football, softball, volleyball, basketball, and hockey. Now, those towns that did have these organizations usually would have six or seven teams that would compete against one another throughout the various seasons. Slowly, that was not good enough for the parents. The players were fine with it. They didn't know any other way; they just knew that they had fun playing sports. Many parents believed that their little boy or little girl "star" was being held back by the remaining players on their team. So they got together and started to select all-star teams from each town at the youth level. This was the beginning of the end for dodgeball and other games that did not need adults to organize them.

The all-star teams that were formed at the end of the season would then play a few games against the surrounding all-star teams. Parents and players were all very happy for a number of years. The parents of these all-stars would make sure that all their friends, family, and neighbors were aware of the fact that their child made the all-star team. And if you didn't hear them the first time, they made sure that the next ten times they bumped into you on the street, they would recall the play-by-play of the big game.

Not everything was all roses, because the bitter political battles soon began. Who would be the head coach of the all-star team, and how many assistants would the coach use during the games? The all-star team had to be composed of players from all ten teams, right? Well, as long as the players were winning, that was the case. Then they would go through a few bad years of all-star results, and someone would bring this issue to the table: "We need to only select the best players in the league; not every team should have representation."

After a few years, the parents' involvement increased exponentially. This meant that the all-star format wasn't good enough for them anymore. They wanted these all-stars to play together throughout the entire season. At that moment, travel sports were born—travel soccer, basketball, baseball, and so on. Each town would still run its league that would provide an opportunity for all children who wanted to play sports, but now, they had another level to strive for called *travel sports*. These teams were performance-based teams, and players would have to try out in order to make the squad. Generally speaking, these travel teams would start around seven years old, which, by the way, in travel sports terms, would be the under-eight age category. Now that the parents were completely consumed with their children's careers, their minds started racing out of control.

Most of the stories that I will share with you in this book occurred during my involvement with youth soccer specifically. The following occurred during a holiday party when my oldest son was ten years old. With my first two children, I tried my best to coach them as they started their young careers. I figured it was the least that I could do, being a NCAA Division I men's soccer coach for fifteen years. This may have led the parents to have some inflated expectations, because they saw their little nine- and ten-year-old players as being trained by a college coach. I am not sure, but the evening of the holiday party, when we were just sitting around talking and having fun, one of the dads came up to me and with a serious face asked, "So what are your expectations for Anton?" I tried to clarify his question by asking what he specifically meant by *expectations*. He went on to say, "I believe, without a doubt, with my son's speed, size, skill, and desire, he should warrant a scholarship when the time comes."

I looked at him and tried to respond both as courteously and as honestly as I could. I started off with the fact that I wanted Anton to have fun and hoped that he developed a passion for the game, because once you have a passion for something, you then have intrinsic self-motivation for whatever you do, which, in turn, will always make you a success in life. I then said that it was almost impossible to determine whether a nine-year-old would one day receive an athletic scholarship. He then mentioned how he and his wife wished that they had started their older son sooner; if so, he probably would have been eligible for money when he went to college.

This way of thinking has been part of our American culture for the past fifteen years. Travel sports evolved naturally, especially because they had so much support from the adults who helped them develop. At this point, the question has to be asked: Exactly how much did the adults cause this evolution, and did that input help or hurt the direction that sports have taken? Either way, you must agree that sports have evolved at an unhealthy pace. I will go as far as to predict that sports are on a fast track to ending up like the white-tailed deer population did in upstate New York.

So, movement toward organized youth sports started to put extreme amounts of pressure on the free time that kids were accustomed to having after school during the week and especially during the weekend. Remember, this free time is very important if our kids are going to learn independence and create things on their own. The parents with good intentions, of course, didn't stop there. We all remember when our mom would throw a birthday party of us, and she would invite all the kids in our class. Those who could make it to the party would come over to our house for a couple of hours to play in the backyard, pin the tail on the donkey, and maybe hit a piñata. Ice cream and cake were served, presents were opened, and then everyone went home. Now, these are weekly occurrences, called *playdates*—all of which parents organize for the sole purpose that their children socialize with their friends in an environment other than school. Anyone figured out why? Because Mom can control the environment that the children play in.

Is that real life? Not a chance. Real life is letting kids head out to recess after lunch, create a game with their friends, organize it, run it, control it, and fight and battle, all of which are critical to a child's ability to develop in our society. The playdate is a wonderful idea, and it has good intentions, but it only holds children back when adults constantly solve all the problems and organize every activity during the day.

Dodgeball is the last wild environment that our kids will ever encounter before they are forced into the adult world. Without dodgeball and games like it, our kids won't be able to keep up with the natural pace of evolution, putting them at a distinct disadvantage to many other cultures around the world. If you haven't figured it out by now, I am very passionate about this topic. This is my passion, and I am doing my best to transfer to you what I believe our future will look like if we let our school districts take away dodgeball for our kids to enjoy and play. As I write this, I have no way of knowing how many of my fellow Americans believe in what I am saying, and I will be forced to wait and see if this book ever even makes it into one bookstore. I have never been afraid of failure, and I won't start now.

Let's continue on with our look at the evolution of youth sports, because it is about to move faster than the speed of light. Premier sports came next, and I myself was directly involved with this development. Only now, six years after I started my own premier soccer program, have I started to ask, "What have I done?" Over the years, as a Division I men's soccer coach in my region, many soccer people would approach me, asking why we didn't have a premier club here. I would always respond with the fact that it is very hard to start one, it takes thousands of hours to develop, and then it's difficult to have success when it's all done.

In 1999, I found myself with about three weeks to kill after having my first open-heart surgery to repair my aortic valve. I decided to try to put together a proposal for our local club to take a look at. After talking with the club president, he and I agreed that it was worth the effort. Many board meetings later, and after about six months of work, the club Middlepath FC was born. Our town club at LaGrange now had every level of soccer to offer our community: in-house, travel, inter-town, and premier. Now, our Hudson Valley region in New York had the premier club that so many of the residents desired. Without realizing it, I now had blood on my hands with regard to the impending extinction of dodgeball. I myself got so caught up in the soccer frenzy, being a college coach and having children of my own who wanted to play soccer at the highest level they could achieve. I was living two separate lives—one, doing my teaching job, where every day I fought to keep dodgeball alive; the other, trying to reach the NCAA Division I tournament with my college team, and also trying to gain national recognition for my newly formed premier soccer club called Middlepath. I never once stopped to take a look at how the two were complete enemies. I was just pushing forward, trying to succeed in both my careers.

So how is it that premier sports are slowly killing dodgeball? Simply stated, being involved with premier sports gives your child the slight chance to someday gain a college or university athletic scholarship. Playing dodgeball is only going to take your child away from the valuable time needed to train your little future Pelé. That's it. Do we, as parents, really believe that our kids are having more fun as we yell at them from the sidelines as they try to gain victory in an adult-run athletic event? Or do they have more fun in a gym with two teams, one referee, and the freedom to create, run, hop, skip, throw, dodge, avoid, and strike with their friends? For those of you whose kids live in a school district that still allows dodgeball, go ask them right now what they have more fun doing. Ask them, "Do you have more fun in gym class playing dodgeball or going to soccer, basketball, gymnastics, or tennis practice?" What they say might shock you. For those of you who live in a school district that has already banned the game, you will never get the opportunity to ask your child the same question. That is very sad. You are being robbed of experiencing a true pleasure with your kids.

Picture never being able to ask your kids, "Hey, honey, what is your favorite cartoon? Do you like Popeye, Scooby-Doo, or SpongeBob?" I realize that every generation is different from the next, but it is very fun when you can link together ideas and topics from generations gone by. Your kids could respond with something like this: "They had Scooby-Doo way back when you were a kid?" You are forever losing out on opportunities to connect with your child.

Please try to remember that not all kids like dodgeball, but the overwhelming majority do. We must always keep this in mind as we continue to look at the other variables that are driving dodgeball off the planet. Again, try to remember that this evolution has taken place over the past twenty-five to thirty years, which is less than a millisecond in our human evolution. We don't know where this is all going to end up. At least the FDA may take as many as ten years to introduce a new medication to our population, only after it has studied the medication from ten thousand different angles. In organized youth premier sports that train and play year-round, we are putting a product out there, with our subjects being young humans, and we have no idea what effect this will have on their futures. We just assume that it is in their best interest, while trying to gain an advantage for our children to compete at the high school and college levels.

Scientists have already determined that young children are developing specific injuries at a much faster rate than in the past. Much of their research has to do with the fact that many young athletes are selecting specific sports to play all year long, and this stresses specific joints and muscle groups beyond the breaking point, resulting in many more injuries. Most sports medicine physicians agree that all these injuries are due to the fact that the kids are not cross-training effectively. For example, they could cross-train by playing soccer in the fall, then playing basketball in the winter. Both sports work different muscle groups and specific joints. My point does not even address what we are already seeing in terms of physical injuries. My concern is how these young children will be psychologically affected, either benefiting from it or missing out on certain aspects of their childhood, due to the intense year-round pressure to compete and succeed in a specific sport.

So, we have taken a quick look at how organized youth sports are affecting the childhood games that many of us played in the past, specifically dodgeball. The next question we have to answer is this: How has this new philosophy injected itself into our public schools in such a short period of time? To answer this question, we need to take an in-depth look at public school administrations and, more specifically, principals and athletic directors. Forty to fifty years ago, very few students attended college with the specific desire to become a high school principal or athletic director. Those positions were usually filled from within the school district as teachers and coaches entered into fifteen to twenty years of service. These teachers would take administration courses at the local teachers college and obtain their administration certificates.

Most of those people who went on to become our principals and athletic directors were teachers who were very good leaders, great motivators, and excellent communicators and were not afraid to make a tough decision when one needed to be made. And almost always, they based that decision on what was best for their students and staff—not on the external pressure that came from the community. So many of these administrators were either gym teachers in the school district or subject-area teachers who had coached in the district for many years. It was only logical that these teachers were very good communicators; they could help groups of people with different points of view find common ground, just as they had done for many years as the head football or basketball coach. More often than not, their colleagues already respected them for the hard work and countless hours that they put into their jobs. In short, the board of education members knew exactly what they were getting when they offered the job to these individuals.

That being said, these people usually had an affinity for dodgeball, and they understood how important it was that the kids play games and blow off some steam. So when that one parent came in to talk about his or her child not enjoying playing dodgeball in gym class, the discussion ended exactly there. They were able to see the parent's point of view, understand his or her concerns, and then reassure the parent that his or her child would be perfectly safe and that he or she had nothing to be concerned about. Problem solved. The next day, such an administrator would stop into the gym to ask the coach how the game went last night and to also casually ask how little Jenny Wallflower was doing in gym class. He might say something like, "Try to make sure that she has fun. She looks a little down." And that would end the conversation.

More often than not, the really great administrators were able to connect with the entire staff about any issues that would come up in the educational setting, always taking the time to look at the situation from the students' point of view, the teachers' point of view, and, of course, the parents' perspective. This was how relationships were developed and built, and how they remained strong into the future. Each individual school in the district had its unique tone when you walked through the front doors. And you could feel it the moment you entered. Discipline was considered the most valuable lesson that any young child could master, and many of those administrators made sure that the student population understood the expectations and, of course, the consequences for their actions when they broke the rules.

The reality today is simple: these administrators started to retire and die. Over time, gradually, what happens to all of us happened to their generation; they were affected by the law of impermanence. This started the crack in the mortar and bricks that soon became the start of dodgeball's decline in our public schools. Boards of education and school districts slowly changed the educational environment as it related to hiring administrators. There began a push for administrators to have doctoral degrees. Well, of course, that started to push many gym teachers out of the running, not because they weren't intelligent enough to obtain their doctorates, but because they refused to take the sixty credit hours necessary to gain the degree. More often than not, schools now advertised the search for a new administrator around the state. And administrator positions often became nationwide searches for what the district believed would be the right fit for the school.

Highly educated, with many degrees, this new-age administrator faced extreme pressure to achieve academic excellence within his or her school and school district. The state began to put more and more pressure on the districts that were underachieving. Every time they faced a budget crunch, districts cut back many classes that children needed to truly be kids. Gym, art, and music—the *specials classes*, as they have always been named—were always on the chopping block when things got tight, all in the pursuit of academic achievement. These new-age administrators became masters of the art of self-preservation.

When people are concerned about their future, they often do things that are in their own, not the organization's, best interest. This is human nature in its most primitive form. Even Neanderthal knew that they needed to keep the clan alive and healthy if they were to survive through the fierce winter. If a strong member of the group were to die during a hunt, that would surely be fatal to the entire group. So they worked together in perfect tandem as they took down the great beasts thousands of years ago. Members were not expendable. Not so anymore.

This isn't meant to be an all-out assault on administration. But when that same parent comes in today to talk about his or her child's experience in gym class as it relates to a specific situation, game, or activity—for example, dodgeball—the administrator does one-third of his or her job very well. He or she will always take the time to look at the situation through the parent's eyes during the meeting. What happens next divides the great administrators from the not-so-great administrators. I apologize for using that politically correct phrase *not-so-great administrators*. What I meant to say is *crap administrators*. Hey, let's be honest and fair. Maybe the gym teacher in question is out of line and the game is very dangerous and it puts the children's safety in jeopardy. That is a simple problem to solve; the administrator points out the parts of the activity that are dangerous, finds a way to work with the teacher to make sure that those parts don't happen again, and we move on. That's simple. But this case isn't simple. This child is just trying to avoid any type of activity that the teacher offers.

In this situation, the administrator has the responsibility to sit down such parents and remind them that their child is heading toward a sedentary existence, and if they continue to make excuses for the child, they will only help the child down a path that will lead to many years of suffering in the future. "Please try to convince your children that it is important for them to participate in this game, as it is necessary for their physical and emotional development." End of discussion.

I also have to be fair to the administration. Over the past ten to fifteen years, a big push for shared decision making in our public schools has taken place. Almost all our public schools in New York now have building-level teams that have been created for shared decision making. These teams often consist of administrators, teachers, parents, students, custodial staff, and so on. I was a founding member of one of my school's building-level teams about fifteen years ago. I was a member for three years, and in that time, we accomplished very little.

The most important teachers in our children's lives are their parents. Every day, one of my kids comes home with a crazy story from school, like one from my thirteen-year-old son, Anton. In health class, his teacher pointed out the difference between 85 percent and 93 percent lean beef. She went on to mention that the 93 percent lean beef was more expensive, but that she would rather spend the extra money now, so that she didn't have to spend the time later in life hooked up to wires and tubes in a hospital bed. These scare tactics are what drive me crazy about our schools today. They just follow the mainstream media's lead. This is where my job as a parent becomes very important. I need to tell my son stories of how his great-grandfather and grandmother used to cook all their food with bacon fat. They would keep a large tin can on the stove and pour all the bacon grease from the morning's breakfast into the can and then use it to cook their eggs and any other foods that they needed to spice up a bit. And then I remind him that they both lived until they were eighty-two years old. So is it more important to have a person who eats only completely healthy foods but has psychological problems because he or she is so stressed out about trying to live this perfect, healthy life? Remember, stress can take you down much faster than a McDonald's cheeseburger.

You already know the antidote for this new-age philosophy: more dodgeball. So this impending extinction couldn't have come at a worse time. At this time, I may only have a handful of colleagues in the public school who still believe that dodgeball is critical, but we are receiving some help from outside the education system. Over the past ten to fifteen years, private organizations have gotten together to help keep dodgeball alive. Four major leagues continue to promote the game by holding regional and national tournaments, local leagues, and clinics and workshops around the country. The largest national dodgeball leagues are the National Dodgeball League (NDL), the National Amateur Dodgeball Association (NADA), the World Dodgeball Association (WDA), and the International Dodgeball Federation (IDBF). These leagues are very important to the long-term promotion of the greatest game on the planet. But the fact remains that these organizations are looked at by the public school systems as convicted sex offenders and are not allowed to be any closer than one mile from any public school around the country.

Let's take a quick look at our colleges and universities and see how they are culpable in the rapid extinction of dodgeball. First of all, due to the ever-increasing work ethic of nations around the world, our American education system is under extreme pressure to catch up with the German, Asian, and Indian education systems in regard to their science and technology departments. So our businesses and corporations are putting pressure on our universities to step up so their graduates have the skills to compete in this global market. That pressure then transfers to our high schools to offer more AP classes for college credit so that high school graduates are ready to tackle university-level challenges. The trickle-down continues. The high schools then put pressure on the middle and elementary schools to focus on accelerating academics during the school day. The school day is only so long. And within that school day, schools must at the very least provide time for children to eat lunch. Many elementary schools are under such pressure that they only allow students about twenty minutes to eat their lunch. They give them another twenty minutes for recess. The only other times during the school day that are not devoted to academics are the special-area classes, such as art, gym, and music.

You may be asking how this directly relates to dodgeball. Well, if you are going to put so much pressure on these young students during the day and not allow them time to have fun, you will create time bombs. So gym class cannot just include skill development, or aerobics, or movement exercise. These gym classes must be made up of activities and games that will allow the children the opportunity to run, jump, skip, throw, catch, compete, win, and lose—exactly what dodgeball creates. So when my ten-year-old son Aiden comes home from school and talks about what he did in gym class today, it almost brings a tear to my eye. But I don't want to be hypocritical. I want to practice what I preach, so I have not called up the school, or the teacher, to ask why my fifth-grade child is doing step aerobics and simple movement for twenty-five minutes and then playing a small game for about five minutes. I must find a way to create an environment that cultivates the evolution of dodgeball so that many of our public schools cannot ignore this exciting environment that helps children through their difficult day and affords them the time that they deserve to be children. In doing so, these school districts may ultimately see these benefits for generations to come.

I alone cannot change the mind of my son's gym teacher or the school's administration, nor do I believe that it is my right to change their minds about anything. This is how many new-age liberals live their lives, convinced that it is their God-given right and duty to change the way that you live, think, work, play, and so on. I am trying very hard to inform as many people as I can by writing this short story about what I see every day. So many teachers across the country are so afraid of change and the possibility that their careers will be cut short that they bite their lip when they communicate with these new-age parents. They often sugarcoat what they see with these parents' children in their classroom. This is sad.

I find it ironic that higher education has inadvertently put such pressure on dodgeball, yet year after year, intramural athletic programs at those same colleges and universities develop dodgeball leagues, tournaments, and pick-up games, just as you would with intramural basketball, volleyball, soccer, and so on. Remember now, these are not Division I athletes playing in these games; students in the schools' general population compete in these tournaments and leagues, all because they realize that they love the game, the game is fun, and within a few short years, they will be forced into the real world to fight for their lives in the workforce.

At this point in my story, I would like to ask you to again reflect on your childhood. Take a few moments to see if you can remember a traumatic or significant situation between you and your parents that happened as a result of who you were as a kid. Take note of how your mom and dad disciplined you and how they were involved with the outcome of that situation. How did that outcome immediately affect you years ago? If they had approached the situation differently, would it have changed the way that you are today? Please try to remember that all parents are human, or were before they passed away, and as humans, it is in our nature to make mistakes, and we will make them every day of our lives. But these mistakes directly affect the outcome of another human's existence.

I apologize if this exercise brings back painful memories. That is not my intention. I want to get you to look at the true nature of the situation that may have occurred over twenty-five years ago and to be honest about how you reacted then and how you would react to the same situation today if you were that kid again. Then attempt to make a judgment on whether that situation helped prepare you for the real world or hurt you in the long run.

CHAPTER 4

Discipline

To really explain what I am asking you to do, I will have to get personal and bring up my past, as I look at it now after twenty-seven years. Growing up in a small town in upstate New York had its benefits and its disadvantages, for sure. I was raised by my mother and father and grew up with three sisters. Both my mom and dad graduated as gym teachers, as did my oldest sister and younger sister. So, five out of six in the family were gym teachers while my other sister loved horses, cows, and farm animals and has followed in my grandparents' footsteps by living on a small family farm. Needless to say, our house was filled with competitive athletes who lived and died by the game. My life was made more interesting when, while attending Middleburgh High School, my high school principal was my father and my gym teacher was my mother, not to mention that my uncle was my math teacher and my aunt was my art teacher. It was a small school, and my sisters and I had no place to hide.

The following situation took place during my junior year in high school while I was playing basketball in the second round of sectionals. Sectionals are a single-elimination tournament that occurs after league play has finished for the season. All teams and players strive to win the sectional tournament so that they get invited to the state tournament. As you already know, I did not need any motivation to compete, nor did I need any more stimuli to germinate the seed of anger that I was born with. The game was back and forth. I had just received my fourth foul of the game, and in my opinion, this foul was not warranted. As I turned to the referee to show my displeasure, he immediately hit me with a technical foul. At this point in my career, I had already earned myself an unfavorable reputation for abusing referees, officials, or any other authority figure involved with sports. In this game, the next foul called on me would be cause for ejection. (Before I continue, I want to make it very clear to you, the reader, that I take full responsibility for my actions from when I was a kid up until the present.)

Thirty seconds later, I stepped in front of the big gun for the other team, attempting to create an offensive-foul situation, but the referee saw it from a completely different point of view and called me for a block. This meant that I had fouled out of the game with more than three minutes to play, which in basketball is an eternity. That was it. In my eyes, this adult had just taken me out of the game unjustly, and being that I was already out of the game, I made sure that I lashed out at this person with as much venom and evil as I could muster up with my limited command of the English language. I ran straight up to him and chest-butted him, which in and of itself could almost be considered assault. But I continued; I told this guy that I would make it my life's mission to find out where he lived and then burn his house to the ground.

At this point, my good friend Timmy pulled me away, and I headed for the bench. In my sixteen-year-old mind, mine had seemed a perfectly legitimate response to what had just occurred. Remember, I was born with the seed of anger and truly feared nothing. We lost the game, and I do remember feeling bad that I must have let the team down by fouling out, but I honestly don't remember my coach ever disciplining me for my actions. As a matter of fact, I don't recall being benched during my high school career in either soccer or basketball. I always benched myself due to my actions against the opponent or the referees.

The next day, school started out very normal with the morning announcements, but when the announcements ended, there was one more to come. "Would Bobby Herodes please come down to the main office?" I thought that was odd. When my father, being the principal, ever needed to talk to me, he would come to my class and call me out into the hall. My mind was at ease; I knew I hadn't done anything wrong as I walked down the long, silent hall to the office.

When I entered the office, the secretary said, "Your father would like to see you behind closed doors." Okay, now my interest was piqued.

As I walked into his office, I saw two New York state troopers standing there. My father asked me to take a seat as my mind raced out of control.

The first trooper started questioning me. "Are you Robert Joseph Herodes, born May 12, 1965?"

I answered, "Yes."

"Is your address RD 1 Schoharie, New York?"

"Yes."

"We are here on behalf of one David Cooper."

My first thought was, *Oh shit, is that the new family that moved in to the old house up on the hill where I was hunting the other day? But wait, I didn't see any posted signs. Maybe he just put them up, and now, I am in deep trouble.* My mind was racing. I knew I shouldn't have gone up there until I got his permission. It was customary for a hunter and trapper to always get permission to harvest any animal on another man's property.

But I was way off base, because the trooper next said, "We are here to investigate the threat to cause harm and cause arson to Mr. Cooper's person and property." I still couldn't put this whole thing together. "Do you recall this threat that was made at approximately 8:45 p.m. last night in the town of Duanesburg?"

What the hell is this guy talking about? I thought. *I was at a sectional basketball game last night and didn't get home until around 10:00 p.m.*

The trooper then asked, "Were you playing in a sectional basketball game last night in the town of Duanesburg?"

"Yes, I was, so how could I have threatened this man named David Cooper when I was playing basketball?"

The trooper responded, "Mr. Cooper was one of the two officials during last night's game."

At that moment, everything seemed to stand still. Time had stopped. *Are these troopers here because I said that I was going to burn this guy's house down?* I thought. I had made tons of somewhat similar threats during my young athletic career, so what was the big deal? *Isn't that what all angry athletes do at one point or another?* My two favorite sportspeople were Bobby Knight and John McEnroe. I would always watch Indiana basketball, and whenever John played in a tennis tournament, I watched the entire match and just waited for him to explode against the linesman or opponent. All these thoughts were running through my mind.

The next statement that the trooper made was "We are going to have to bring you in for fingerprinting and formally charge you with aggravated *something or other.*" I couldn't remember the charge but heard that they wanted me to go with them to the police barracks to be charged with this crime. But first, they asked me to sit outside my father's office for a few minutes.

As I sat in the hallway for those three or four minutes, I finally understood what fear was. It was horrible. I immediately felt sick to my stomach; my heart was pounding out of my chest, and I started sweating while sitting in the cold, damp tile hallway. Time and again, my father had mentioned that, one day, I would push it too far and that I would have a criminal record, and once you have a record, it changes your life forever. My father, having been the principal of the school for about six years, was always working with the state troopers, and of course knew both these guys because they had come to the high school countless times due to fights and drug issues.

When they called me back into the office, the troopers said that they were going to release me into my father's authority; having worked with my dad, they felt fairly confident that he would take care of punishing me with severity while making sure that I did not get officially charged with a crime. I had never felt such relief as I did at that very moment. Just two minutes before, my life had taken a turn for the worse due to my own actions. I had no one to blame but myself and my uncontrollable emotions. But just as soon as my life seemed doomed, in the next second, I was reborn after hearing the troopers recommend that I be released into my father's authority. For once in my life, I felt so happy that my father was my high school principal and that I would not have a criminal record.

More often than not, being the son of my high school principal sucked. Every day of my high school career, some kid would come up to me and say, "Your father is the biggest assh— in the world, and one of these days, I'm gonna get him back." My response was always the same: "Go ahead, try to kick his ass, and see where it gets you." My dad was about six foot one, 210 pounds, and pure muscle everywhere. Having grown up on a farm, my father had forearms the size of most high school students' thighs. At the same time, I knew that this punishment was going to be bad, and that I would probably be grounded for some time to come. But I said to myself I had finally learned my lesson, I had dodged a huge bullet, and I would never behave that way again.

My father chose a way to solve this problem. His intentions were good, and at that moment, as a sixteen-year-old kid, I thought the decision to take control of the situation and take it out of the New York State police's authority was very good. Did this method of discipline work for me over twenty-six years ago? I wish I could tell you that it did. But it didn't. I would encounter many similar situations during my childhood and college years—some less severe, some more severe. All I know is that I continued on this path of having to win at all costs, and I would do whatever it took, whether it meant abusing my body, the opponent, the officials, or even my own teammates. I needed to win, and I would sacrifice anything and everything in my power to do it.

This life philosophy would often leave me lonely with very few friends, and always with a sense of guilt for what I had just done. This guilt would build up over the years and become so heavy that it grew unbearable at times. I can remember not sleeping at all, constantly reliving what had happened during the game and how I had reacted. I was cursed with two personalities—one when I was competing and one when the game or contest was over. When I wasn't competing, I was always joking, laughing, having fun, and enjoying other people's company. As a matter of fact, one of the things that I liked to do during my childhood was to help my friends and other students who were having trouble with relationships and issues. I always seemed to be able to solve everyone's problems, but never really could see the fact that I myself had a huge anger problem. Life was great. But when I stepped back into the arena, there was no joking allowed.

Now, as an adult looking back on that situation that happened twenty-six years ago, I can clearly see the truth of how my parents might have handled that incident. I love my parents, and I would never criticize any of their decisions in raising me, because we, as parents, always want what is best for our kids, but more often than not, we do what we think is best in the moment. It takes a lot of wisdom to be able to see into the future and make educated predictions on what is best for your child. Those educated predictions become easier when you understand the true nature of each and every child. And that understanding only comes from connecting with those children at a very young age. So remember, as a parent, you should already know the personality of each individual and know which child has the seed of anger, which has the seed of fear, and so on. So what might be right when you are disciplining a child who is afraid of his own shadow will not work at all on a child who fears nothing, like myself.

So let's say that my parents truly understood my existing anger, especially when it came to athletics. Allowing the New York state troopers to handcuff me and take me down to their station, fingerprint me, book me, and possibly have me spend the night in a holding cell may have been the better decision at that moment in time. Undoubtedly, that would have been very traumatic for any sixteen-year-old, but that twenty-four hours of trauma may have forced me into realizing that I had a problem with my emotions. And because of that trauma, I may have gained some important insight into my life as a sixteen-year-old kid that could have saved me countless sufferings that occurred after my sixteenth year of life. We can never know for sure if that would have been the case. All that I am asking you to do is to have awareness of the fact that as parents and teachers, we make decisions every moment of every day. If we are to be the best parents that we can be, we must take a moment to think about the decisions that we are going to hand out and how those decisions will possibly affect our children in the present and the future.

Now that I have shared with you one of my life experiences, I hope that you will take a look at an experience that happened during your childhood and see how a different decision might have affected you into your teen years and young adulthood.

Since the evolution of mankind, humans have played games at young and old ages, games that had consequences when one team didn't perform as well as the other team. We humans never played games where every kid won. There were never races where every sprinter received a ribbon. Those games that we played gave our kids chances to find out who they were, not only as athletes but as social beings on this earth.

Dodgeball may already seem dead in many of our towns across the country. But it is slowly evolving and struggling to survive in this ever-changing environment. Don't take away your children's opportunity to discover who they are on their own. Then and only then will they have that enlightened moment when they realize what they are meant to do on this earth, and when they discover it on their own, they will have complete ownership of it and be able to develop the passion that they need to succeed in our global economy for generations to come. So the next time your children come home with a scratch on their knee or elbow, investigate what happened. Make sure that the incident was due in part because they are children. Put some Bactine on the wound, give them a hug and kiss, and tell them that sometimes in life they will get hurt. Then send them off to do their homework or whatever other family traditions that you have created in your household. (Please don't call your local elementary, middle, or high school to ask that changes be made so that your children will never get hurt again.) This type of support will allow me and other gym teachers around the country to make sure that dodgeball continues to evolve and stay healthy for many more generations to come.

CHAPTER 5

Funball

At this point in my short story, I would like to thank you for taking some of your valuable time to look at one man's view as to why dodgeball is very near extinction. And now, I am looking for your honest opinion of the game I have created that has slowly evolved from dodgeball over the past seventeen years.

At the beginning of the book, I mentioned that I had an exciting game to talk to you about. That exciting game is called *Funball*—although it wouldn't become officially named *Funball* until ten years after I created it. This evolution started as a result of some pressure that I was receiving as an elementary school gym teacher. Sometimes, the pressure came from a photocopied article about a school district being sued by a family over a dodgeball injury, which someone placed on my desk. Or it came from a subtle comment one of my administrators made in walking through my gym to get to the stage, where all our PA systems were stored. As a result of this pressure I felt, I started doing some research on the Internet about dodgeball and how it was doing around the Northeast.

Years ago, and to a certain degree today, school districts developed and implemented their own curriculum when it came to gym, art, music, and so on. Even seventeen years ago, some school districts were forcing gym teachers to change their curriculum to eliminate dodgeball.

Dodgeball was the greatest of childhood games, which we have already discussed at length. But from a curriculum and skill standpoint, dodgeball had throwing, catching, dodging, and movement as its basic skills that the kids used while playing. During my research, I realized that I needed to develop the game so that it incorporated many more curriculum skills and concepts so that I could force the administration to realize that this game was multidimensional, not one-dimensional.

Now, as I watched my kids play dodgeball, I was studying the game in a way that I never had before. And one day, when I was teaching a kindergarten class, inspiration came to me. These kids were five years old, and their throwing skills were horrible. Most of the children's throws rarely made it to the other side of the gym, even though my gym was only about sixty feet long by forty feet wide. Only three or four students in the class could throw the ball hard enough to eliminate players. Games would go on forever, and the weak, unskilled students never got the chance to eliminate an opponent. How could I increase the excitement of the game while making sure that all the players in the game were capable of achieving success, speeding up the game, and, most important, keeping it safe?

After about one week of studying the game with every ounce of my brain, the solution finally came to me. It had been right there under my nose the entire time, but I only truly noticed it when the kindergarten and first-grade students were playing. The rule that changed dodgeball forever was created: "All balls are live." I told the kids that even if someone rolled a ball across the floor and it touched their sneaker, they were out. A bouncing ball, a rolling ball, a stationary ball—they were all live. And if a player didn't pick up a ball cleanly or bobbled and dropped it, he or she was out. It was amazing. My fifth-grade students showed some resistance, but they quickly fell in line, and dodgeball started to evolve that same day. Now, the game was multidimensional.

All kids need to practice and master the very important skill of tracking an object, not only in the gym, but in all forms of life, and now, players were forced to track the flight of the ball after it left the thrower's hand and also after it passed them and rebounded off the back wall, side wall, other teammates, ceiling lights, and basketball rims.

Players now had to memorize and utilize the entire dodgeball court if they were going to become good at the game. Players who used to stand in the corners to avoid being hit were now in danger of a rebound shot off the back or side wall. If you were one of those risk-taking kids who would try to field the bouncing ball or the ball thrown into the air, you were living on the edge. The more conservative players would let the ball fly by them and then pick it up after it had rebounded off the back wall, almost coming to a complete stop. Now, the players had to incorporate the grounding and fielding skills used in baseball and softball. Without even knowing it, kids were starting to use geometry— angles and trajectories of the balls. Some of the skilled players would try to purposely throw a ball off the side wall to eliminate a player. There seemed to be no end in sight to the kids' creations while playing the game all because of that simple rule change that all the balls were live all the time.

Now remember, this all took place while I was working at a K–5 elementary school. All these strategies and creations were coming from the minds of young children. The smart players, or, as I nicknamed them, the *brains*, would never throw a ball in the air at an opponent. Those players would always ricochet the ball off the floor just before the opponent's legs. This ball was very hard to avoid, and this strategy was brilliant because the enemy could never catch their ball out of the air to eliminate them. Those kids who would huddle up together to try to find safety in numbers became easy targets for the enemy. And more often than not, double and triple kills would occur because the ball would bounce from player to player in their tight little pack. You think a triple play in baseball is exciting; well, it doesn't even compare to the joy kids feel when they get a triple kill in Funball.

The next rule change we adopted was also revolutionary but so simple. I called it *sneak and steal*. I allowed students to sneak over to the other team's side of the court and steal a ball that was across the black line. But by doing this, the students were also taking a big risk, because any player on the other side of the gym could just run up and tag the player with his or her hand to eliminate them. The sneak-and-steal rule really opened up the game and now incorporated a chasing, fleeing, and tagging aspect to the game.

With two seemingly simple rule changes, the game had completely changed and incorporated more than fifteen different curriculum skills, concepts, and standards. This game now had it all, but as any good creator knows, there is always room for improvement. Every morning, I would walk into the gym wondering what new twists the kids would put into the game. To the untrained eye, this game was still dodgeball. Any administrator or athletic director who came into the gym and saw the kids throwing balls at each other would just assume that they were playing dodgeball. But it couldn't have been further from the truth. This new game was not dodgeball; this game was awesome.

At the end of every class, I would give the entire class the opportunity to play against me in one more game before they left the gym. The kids would scream and point their fingers at me, saying that this was the day that they would beat me. One by one, I would pick them off, smiling and laughing the entire time. I was the biggest kid in the gym. I can still remember the day that one of my second-grade classes beat me in the final game. I took my eye off a bouncing ball, and it slipped through my fingertips. The kids rushed the floor to celebrate their victory over the old man.

The next rule to help dodgeball on its rapid evolutionary path was called the *wall-ball rule*. If any player threw a ball the entire length of the dodgeball court and that ball hit the back wall without touching another player or the floor, the thrower was out. The wall-ball rule forced the players to aim low or else risk being eliminated. Safety and fun were always my main concerns when it came to my kids. As a result, I started to implement simple rules that eliminated *headhunting*—or *head shots*, as they were also called—and this simple modification to the rules of dodgeball virtually eliminated the head shot at the elementary level. I created one more rule modification strictly for safety, and this rule was called *excessive force*. If a player used excessive force to eliminate an opponent, I could call that player out, and the player who was hit could remain in the game. I told the kids that while they played the game, not only did I watch and referee, but I also was able to look into the eyes and mind of every player. If I were to see even the slightest touch of anger in a player's eyes while he or she threw a ball at the opponent, I could immediately remove him or her from the game. Communicating this to my kids let the killers and the jocks know that they were being watched at all times for any head shots or excessive-force violations and that they needed to play the game with a happy heart, not an angry one. It also assured the wallflowers that there would be justice during this game and that this little bit of support would help many of them get involved.

This game soon became the model for discipline and honor. It was real-life war right in my gym. And all my kids knew that they had to play it a certain way, or else they would not play it at all. Right now, you may be saying to yourself that I was hypocritical to ask these kids to play a certain way, and that all the creativity that I talked about was being stunted by the discipline that it required to play my game. This is where you have to understand the minds of young humans. To truly be creative, you must be given certain limits. For example, if I put a child in a room filled with objects large and small, short and tall, of all different colors and asked this child to create a new toy, the child would need to use very little effort in the creation because he or she had so many resources available. Now, if I put that same child in a small room with three tongue depressors, a piece of yarn, and a cotton ball and gave him or her the same task as before, that child would have to sit there and study every item ad nauseam until he or she was forced to truly become creative in developing a toy.

So as far as Funball goes, these children were creating every single day, with very little room for error, and that is what made the game so special. Any kid can run around a gym, acting like an idiot, during class if his or her actions have no consequences. I have seen it many times before when I have been at my children's friends' birthday parties. Every time one of my kids comes home with a birthday-party invitation, it gives me an uneasy feeling in the pit of my stomach. And the first thing that my wife says to me, not the kids, before we go into the party is "You better be good today and mind your own business."

So many parents in my generation suddenly go deaf, dumb, and blind when they are around other people's kids. They see all the misbehaving, screaming, fighting, and tantrums, yet they slowly look the other way and walk out of the room. Correct me if I am wrong, but I remember being yelled at by any adult who was near me anytime that I misbehaved—not to mention that if my parents were in earshot when another adult was disciplining me, I got the wooden spoon twice as hard when we got home. I can even remember strangers telling me to shut up, and my first thought was *Who the hell are you?* but I didn't dare speak those thoughts when I was little—because my parents reinforced it. I shut up and tried to get away from them as fast as I could.

Today's parents are doing the exact opposite. And as a result, the children question the adults to see their proper identification and ask, "What certification do you have to tell me what to do? Have my parents given you the proper authority to discipline me at this juncture?" These are actual questions that kids have asked me in the past during my gym classes.

I realize at times my ability to stay on task is not good, and I apologize. Let's get back to the story.

As the kids created while playing the game, I was always trying to create new and different ways of playing Funball. Pin Funball and Basket Funball were very simple to create and easy for the kids to play. I needed to make the game more strategic for my older kids. Prison Funball was the next great variation. Now when hit or eliminated, kids were forced to run into a prison located behind the enemy's territory and stay in prison until one of their teammates would throw them a ball, or a ball would bounce into the prison. Then they had to eliminate an opponent while still in prison before they could come back to their team, while the player they just eliminated was forced to travel across the gym and enter the opposing team's prison. This game produced cross fire with lots of exciting action, plus many laughs for the teacher.

Blob dodgeball was created one day, and as a result, thousands of kids not only had loads of fun running from the giant blob ball, but also had nightmares for many years during their elementary school days. I would only play the game after I told this horrific story of how a meteorite fell from the sky with the tiny blob inside, only for the blob to grow and grow by eating hundreds of animals and people while on its way to Los Angeles. I have had over one hundred kids in the past three years come up to me at the high school and sarcastically thank me for creating endless nightmares for them while they were young. I take it as a compliment, and why not? It means that I am a pretty good storyteller. I have only told the story about five thousand times in the past seventeen years.

The next phase of evolution came when I started to combine completely separate games—such as capture the chicken and dodgeball. What a game. Capture-the-chicken dodgeball was so much fun, and it incorporated so many of the standards that administrators were always talking about. Not only did you have to avoid being eliminated by the dodgeballs that the enemy threw at you, but you also had to guard your chicken and watch out for opponents as they would sneak over to your side of the gym to capture your chicken and run, or throw it back to their team. All the young human beings' senses were being used at the same time. I won't lie to you; this game was very difficult to officiate, and I would sometimes get dizzy looking back and forth from each chicken coop. But it was worth the effort to see the smiles and laughter that continued nonstop during the game. Sure, none of the kids liked being in the prison when they were tagged or hit by the dodgeball. But when they were freed from jail, it was all worth the wait.

CHAPTER 6

Ax Murderer

The holidays were very special to me when I was a kid, so I needed to create versions of dodgeball that would be special to the kids during each holiday. In these competitive games, teams of two players would chase, tag, and throw the dodgeball at the remaining students until every student was eliminated. I would time how long it took each team of two players to eliminate the remaining students in the class. And after all the teams had taken their opportunity to hunt the class, I would tally up the scores, from the slowest time to the fastest, and then crown the champion for every class that I had for that day. These games were special, so they were only played one time during the school year. That bit of information is important to know, because in a little while, I will tell you one of the greatest stories that I have been associated with in my career.

Of course, holding true to my tradition, I would tell a story to set the stage before we would play each game for Halloween, Thanksgiving, Christmas, Valentine's Day, and St. Patrick's Day—all the days that were so special to the little ones throughout the school year. I made up special names for all my holiday games, but I always had a special fondness in my heart for my Halloween game. I named my Halloween dodgeball game *Ax Murderer*. I started the story off by reminding the kids that very strange things always happen on Halloween night and that they need to be extra careful when they go trick-or-treating because of what horrible event happened twenty years ago in a small town in the mountains of Pennsylvania. At this time, I could have heard a pin drop onto the gym floor. The story was so horrible that I would sometimes pause and ask the kids if they thought they could handle the story. They would erupt, screaming, "Tell the story, tell the story!"

I would say, "OK, only if you are sure that you won't be too scared," and continue the following story.

It was a cold evening that Halloween twenty years ago in the small town of Pittsgrove, Pennsylvania, which, by the way, is only about 125 miles from Chappaqua. Up until that night, forty-seven people lived in the small farming town. Things changed forever that Halloween when two fourteen-year-old twins, a brother and sister, while sleepwalking, massacred the entire town. It was one of the worst crimes in Pennsylvania history.

By this time, the kids' eyes were wide-open and their jaws had hit the floor. But, of course, I wouldn't stop there. I went on to mention that to this day, the twins had never been brought to justice. They just seemed to disappear into the woods, never to be seen again. I pointed out that if they were still alive, they would be about thirty-seven years old today.

I would ask questions like, "Do any of you kids have woods in your backyards?" Half the class would raise their hands. Then I would say that most of the woods behind their houses weren't "real" woods with lots of trees and bushes and things like that where people could hide. Some of the tough kids in the class would call out and say that they owned two acres of woods behind their house and there were millions of trees in those woods. How the kids' faces looked determined how much further I would go with the story.

After the story, we would re-enact that Halloween night. The kids would yell as if they were being chased all around the gym by the twin brother and sister. At the end of the class, if I noticed any kids still seemed frightened about the story, I would call them over and ask them if they could keep a huge secret and promise to tell no one for as long as they lived. They would always nod, assuring me of their honesty. Then

I would tell them that I had made up the whole story about the twins, the town, and all the people. They would breathe a sigh of relief as they walked out of the gym, and for years to come, I would remind them in the halls to never tell our secret to anyone.

Every year, I would get about ten to fifteen phone calls from parents, pleading with me to tell their child that the story was not true. No matter how many of these kids I told that I created my stories, they still had nightmares after many of the scary stories that I would tell during the school year.

Let me make a quick point about nightmares and how I see them for young children. It is a fact that all humans who have the ability to dream will one day in their lives have a nightmare. Some children who are more fearful will naturally have more nightmares. It doesn't take a scientist to figure this out. But in my opinion, if children are going to have nightmares, they should have them when they are young and growing up so that it gives their parents the opportunity to help them through their nightmares and fears that follow them every day. It is in the true nature of our minds to have dreams, and sometimes, those dreams are wonderful, and sometimes, those dreams are horrible, just like every day in life. Some are great, and some flat-out suck.

As a parent, if you truly care about your children's complete development, you will take the time to guide your kids through their nightmares and give them techniques to deal with them when they occur. How would you like it if your children had their first nightmare while in college after they had just come back from a fraternity party, living by themselves over ten hours away from home? That is a recipe for disaster. So, from my point of view, yes, nightmares are not pleasant, but they give you another opportunity to teach your children about life and how difficult it can be at times.

Now, the real funny story can be told. I think it was Halloween of 2002, and I was playing with one of my third-grade classes. Our school counselor came into the gym to pull out one of his students for a meeting. This particular student, if I remember correctly, had anger issues similar to mine, and he was not happy being pulled out of gym class to sit down with the counselor and talk about how things were going. As the counselor and student were settling in for their session, the counselor noticed that the student was very angry. The counselor asked him why he was exceptionally angry today during their session— "angrier than I have seen you in quite some time," the counselor said.

The student looked at him as if he had two heads and said, "You're damn right I am angry. Do you know what game you just pulled me out of in gym class?"

The counselor replied, "It just looked like one of Mr. Herodes's games that you have played before."

The student answered back, "Mr. Herodes only plays that game one time every year ... *only one time a year.*"

The counselor asked, "What's so special about this game?"

The student answered, "We were just starting to play Ax Murderer."

The counselor almost fell off his chair when he heard the name of the game. "What did you say that Mr. Herodes calls this game?"

"*Ax Murderer.* We run around the gym with the dodgeballs and try to massacre the entire town as fast as we can, but what do you care, because I have to sit here and talk to you about nothing."

The counselor then sprinted about twenty yards down the hallway, straight for the main office. He asked if the principal was aware of a game that I played called *Ax Murderer.* My principal responded, "Herodes plays a million crazy games, but I would have remembered a game called *Ax Murderer* if I had observed him playing it with the kids."

About a minute later, both my principal and assistant principal were staring through the little square window that all gym doors have, their heads squeezed together, looking at the kids playing Ax Murderer. I waved over to the door for them to both come in and watch the game. They walked in very slowly, looking to the right and to the left as they approached me. They then asked if they could talk with me for a few minutes in the main office. I looked at my new gym partner, who had just started working at the school in September, and asked him to take over solo for a few minutes. We had started team teaching together just a few weeks before.

As I sat down in the office, they closed the door. Now, I was wondering, *What the hell is going on?* I started the conversation with "What's up, guys? Great Halloween so far. What do you think?"

"*Yeah*, about that, Bob. We were just talking with the school counselor, and he stated that one of his students mentioned that every year, you play a Halloween game called *Ax Murderer*. Do you play a game called *Ax Murderer*?"

"I sure do. It is one of the greatest games of the year."

"How long have you been playing this game?"

"About eleven years."

After I said, "About eleven years," I saw the blood drain out of both their faces as we sat in the office. "In light of all the horrible things that have happened on school campuses over the past few years, do you think that we should be playing a game called *Ax Murderer*?"

"Look," I said, "these kids live for this game, and especially the story that I tell them every year."

"Story—you tell a story about the game?"

"I sure do. It is one of my scariest stories that I tell all year. I tell the kids about a brother and sister who, while sleepwalking, massacred an entire town in the hills of Pennsylvania." As I started talking about the story, they both started fidgeting in their chairs, and I could tell that they were worried about damage control. From my point of view, no damage had been done—only great memories and a fun game for kids to play on a very special day called *Halloween*.

On that day, another great American tradition was taken away from our children forever. I am not foolish enough to believe that my game called *Ax Murderer* had become a great American tradition in only eleven years. That's not what I mean. I mean the American tradition of taking kids to special places, letting their minds run wild with amazement, taking them to places that frighten them, and allowing them the opportunity to come out alive on the other side. A great American pastime was gone. Storytelling would never be the same. I now needed to filter my every word to make sure that the shock value, or the fear ratio, or the unbelievability factor was acceptable to the entire population of the school, community, county, state, and country. Again, one of human beings' great motivating factors was taking over me: fear, the fear that some parent would come into the school and make a gym game called *Ax Murderer* an issue.

At the time, I didn't even bother to tell both my administrators that I had talked to many parents over the years about the blob and Ax Murderer. Some conversations with the parents were hilarious as their kids attempted to tell them the story of the blob or Ax Murderer at the dinner table. And during other conversations, I needed to assure the parents that this game would not harm their child in any way physically or emotionally, and I guaranteed that their kid would have a great experience.

This talk with my administrators was just another arrow straight into the heart of dodgeball that was slowly bleeding the game to death. And as dodgeball was bleeding, many other institutions were slowly bleeding—institutions that had made our country the greatest country in the world. Our diversity had made our country so great, but it was slowly turning into an ultrasensitive society that could no longer celebrate our differences and became offended by those who were different from ourselves. My father's family was of full Czechoslovakian descent; my mother was three-quarters German and one-quarter Irish. None of it mattered; we were 100 percent American.

This would be the year that I would officially strike *dodgeball* from my vocabulary. And it was one of the hardest things that I ever had to do. One winter morning, I found another article in my mailbox at school about another family that was suing a school district over a dodgeball situation. I almost snapped that day. Remember, I have an anger issue, and I have been working on cultivating it and keeping it to a minimum. But this day, it was too powerful. As I walked out of the gym to grab a bite to eat, I talked to myself all the way to the teachers' lounge.

As I previously said, I had just started team teaching with another gym teacher, a big kid who loved to play games as much as I did. Now, there were two heads working together, trying as hard as we could to keep our great game alive. When I came back from lunch, my good friend said, "Give it up; it's over. You have fought a good battle, but it is over. We will no longer play dodgeball again within these four walls. Dodgeball is officially dead to us. We will now play Funball."

"Funball—what the hell are you talking about?" I asked.

He went on to say, "Ever since I came here to work with you, we have been playing a totally different game of dodgeball than I have ever played before. These people don't want dodgeball. So we won't give them dodgeball. We will teach them Funball. That is the new official name. *Funball* is better; it's fun."

I said, "I know you are just trying to cheer me up, but I really don't think that I have the energy to start something new at this stage in my career."

He said, "What other options do you have? You have said it to me over one thousand times that if administration took away dodgeball, you would resign on the spot."

I thought about it for a few seconds, and that was it. As each class entered the gym that day, we gave the kids the bad news that dodgeball had died and we would never play another game of dodgeball in this gym as long as we were teachers there. The kids were shocked, to say the least. But we were quick to point out that we had created an even better game than dodgeball and it was called *Funball*. And we said from that day forward, if any student were to use the word *dodgeball*, he or she would feel both of our wraths.

For the next four years, we worked as hard as we could to change one of our nation's greatest establishments. The kids adapted very quickly to the new name of the game. It was my co-teacher and I who had all the trouble in adapting to the new name. It got so bad at one point in the beginning that we vowed that if either of us were to slip up and say the word *dodgeball* before, during, or after school, the other person would get a free shot with a *tinikling stick* (a half-inch thick, four-foot piece of solid maple) to the back of the offender's leg. Or we could choose the punishment of being hit with a tennis ball as hard as it could be thrown at point blank, just not in the face. Having played so much dodgeball with my kids over the years, I found it a monumental challenge to change the name and stick with it even when administration continued to remind us that it was still just dodgeball. We never let it get to us that so many people continued to see my new game as dodgeball. Hey, Rome wasn't built in a day.

Those next few years produced so many great times for the kids in our gym, and it seemed like we were really making a difference. After fourteen years of working with elementary-age students, I desired to see just how much of a difference we had made in the lives of these young students. At this point in my career, I was teaching the little ones all day and coaching the men's soccer program at Marist College, so I had very little contact with the kids once they left my elementary school and moved on to high school. At the end of every school year, when the fifth-grade students would leave my school, I reminded them to try to hold on to the passion for gym class, because as they got older, their priorities would change. I told them, "Please try to remember back to when you were younger and you enjoyed all the games that we played here."

Everyone in our business knew the natural evolution of children as it related to gym class. They would start out as little kindergarten students who were on the ground more than on their feet during class. Then, by the time they got to third and fourth grade, they would play like maniacs in the gym. They had no boy–girl issues; they were just eight- and nine-year-old kids. Then they would move on to the middle school, and in about seventh grade, the kids would start to notice the opposite sex, and as a result, things got sort of funny when it came to competing in coed classes. Don't get me wrong; the jock and the killer still just saw their competitors as the enemy, regardless of whether they were girls or boys. But other students would not compete as hard as they did when they were younger.

Then the kids would move on to the high school, and gym class became a complete bore for more than 75 percent of those kids. Still some students would enjoy certain aspects of that level of gym class, but more often than not, most of the girls wanted nothing to do with changing their clothes and competing during the school day. And by now, some of the jocks were too cool to play in gym class, or they were worried about the big game that night, so they wouldn't play hard during class. So there was a great divide at the high school level, and to get kids motivated, the teacher had to be a magician. Most high school gym teachers would always sing the same tune: "The kids don't want to be here, and it is driving me nuts."

Now, I needed to find out what the true driving force was behind the evolution of kids as it related to gym class, and the only way to do this was to transfer to the high school and witness it for myself. My transfer to the high school was not an easy process, to say the least, due to my school district's policies on current staff and transfers, but I won't bore you with the details. I was finally granted a transfer one week before school opened up for the 2005 school year. Here was my opportunity to finally take a look at the true nature of teenagers as it related to gym class. What factors continuously led these children down the same path of indifference toward gym class as they got older?

I had the unique opportunity to see this from a developmental and emotional standpoint as well. I had already built relationships with all my kids; I got to know most of their personalities when they were little. I had already identified the jocks, brains, dodgers, and so on. I had been teaching in the school district for fourteen years, and four of those fourteen years were spent traveling between two of the three elementary schools. I had taught almost two-thirds of the school's population when they were in grades K–5. For each class of twenty-eight students at the high school, I had already taught ten to twelve of the students years ago.

When I received my schedule, I saw that I would be teaching mostly ninth-grade students with one or two senior classes as well. The curriculum was pretty straightforward: fitness, volleyball, hockey, strength conditioning, racquetball, paddleball, and pickleball. The senior class was called Lifetime Skills and sort of combined health, CPR, and a number of health-related labs that the kids would do throughout the semester.

After the first few weeks, I noticed all the classic signs of kids who were not happy—kids who had the weight of the world on their shoulders. They would walk into the gym building with their backpacks filled with about 150 pounds of books, head down, shoulders slumped, dragging their feet on their way to the locker room. Most of these kids did not want to be here.

During my transfer and in the beginning, many people and friends had warned me to stay away from dodgeball with the students, and my response was always the same: "I don't play dodgeball; I play Funball." I must be honest with you; I felt a little apprehensive about playing any of my old games with the students. What if they had totally forgotten about the blob and capture the chicken and no longer had a passion for dodgeball? Remember, these kids didn't know about the death of dodgeball. When they were in elementary school with me, I still called the game *dodgeball*. So they were totally in the dark about the revolution that my buddy and I had started four years ago. I needed to start all over again. I needed to tell the kids about the tragic end of dodgeball and how it was gone forever, but that out of its ashes rose a game that was ten times more exciting and more creative than dodgeball; it required strategy as well as ability, and of course, every level of student could see success in the arena.

I think it was the third week of school when I decided the time had come to give it a shot. I told one of my ninth-grade classes that we would not be jogging on the track today. I was going to take them back about six years, to when they were in the third grade and played Pin Funball. By the time that class was over, any fear that I had melted away. These kids remembered, they had passion, and they still knew how to laugh.

These kids were so overprogrammed that they didn't otherwise have any time to be kids. They would save up their energy to use it mainly on their academics because they were well aware of the fact that high grades might correlate with admission to the college of their choice. All children face this indisputable fact in school—and have faced it for many years. The difference now is that these kids are so focused on their day-to-day schedules that they have no built-in time to have fun. So it is our jobs as parents and teachers to make sure that they do have that time.

If humans were meant to work every waking moment of their lives, their brains would have evolved differently. Most of the kids in our high school don't even build in time to have lunch during the day. They schedule an extra AP class that takes up the slot that they would have used for lunch. They are so focused on the future that they completely miss the art of living in the moment. That completely goes against the evolution of being a child. Children's minds are built to stay in the moment. Once kids become adults, the mind then takes on the capability to plan, worry, schedule, and organize their lives so that they may become successful and attain the American dream.

Well, the American dream is based on being happy and free to live how you want to live. People cannot accomplish happiness by getting rich, owning real estate, and becoming famous. If that were the case, you would not read about all the tragedies that occur to people across our country after they have won multimillion-dollar lotteries. You wouldn't see all these famous young singers, actors, and athletes in trouble every day in the news. Happiness comes from the ability to live in the moment and enjoy what you have, where you live, and who you spend your time with. You'll only attain true happiness when you learn how to see the true nature of life.

For example, the next time that you feel yourself becoming angry, sad, anxious, or nervous, chances are you are holding on to something from your past. Or your mind is somewhere in the future, concerned about something that is about to happen. Even as you are reading these words in this book, your mind may flash back to something that happened today that made you very angry or sad. Take a good look at that situation that occurred today, and see if you created it by holding on to something, or being repulsed by or adverse to the situation that occurred. All these moments in our lives cause us to suffer. The only antidote for this suffering is to try to stay in the moment, which, by the way, is very hard to do.

These high school kids had played volleyball for about a month every year for the past eight years during gym class, but they had not played Blob Funball for more than eight years. When they started running around the gym, fleeing from the blob and trying to stay alive, they became lost in the moment and, as a result, started having fun. And once I saw these high school students running around laughing while playing the game, I found myself living in that same moment with them. As a teacher, there is no greater sight than when your students smile and enjoy themselves. These teenagers had just as much passion now as they had when they were eight years old. The only thing that had changed was they faced such great pressure to succeed that they no longer wanted to play the traditional sports or activities that they had done for their gym careers. They wanted to have fun. The kids had not changed; you still had your wallflowers, your jocks, and so on. They were just older, and they needed an opportunity to drop their book bags and play a game that gave them freedom of expression and an opportunity for cardiovascular activity, teamwork, and, most of all, fun.

As the school year pushed on, every chance I could get, I would throw out one of the old games that I used to play with my elementary students. Within a few months, that's all the kids wanted. But I had the curriculum to follow, so I had to be careful not to deviate too far from the program designed for the ninth graders. At about the same time, during one of the school staff meetings, someone mentioned that we would need to come up with a new gym class elective that students could choose, because we had lost an elective due to a staff member transferring to another school in the district. At our school, the kids were able to sign up for electives, very similar to how students can in college. I told the staff that I had an idea, but that it would take me a little while to put it together.

I proposed my idea to the other gym teachers in the department, and with some help, I was able to put together a proposal to bring before the chairpersons' meeting at the high school. Twice a week, all the chairs would get together with the principals and meet to discuss various issues with running the school. They were going to hold a special meeting where I would stand up and propose my new elective gym class for our students.

When I stood up, I first told the panel, "I am going to take you back to your childhood. Stay with me for a minute, and you will see how I believe that this elective will benefit our students physically, emotionally, intellectually, and socially."

As I began to talk about Funball, I noticed some strange looks come across the faces of the faculty members in the room. Then I started naming the other games that the students would be playing, such as capture the pig, the blob, and so on. Some of the people smiled and laughed at all the wacky names that I had created over the years. At this point, the decision could have gone either way. In the end, they agreed to allow me to give it a go and to put together my curriculum, and they would then place my elective in the Decisions catalog, which the kids used to select their classes for the next year. I called my elective Games: The Color of Life.

At the same time that I was proposing my new class to the chairpersons, I was also trying to get a schoolwide Funball tournament started. After asking my director of athletics and getting a lukewarm response at best, I decided to just focus on the new class for next year and leave it at that. About two weeks later, some junior students from one of the high school clubs approached me about holding a Funball tournament. I gave them the bad news that I had just attempted to do the same thing a few weeks ago, and it had blown up like the *Hindenburg*. I told them to give it a shot but not to get their hopes up. They came back the next day and said they had gotten the okay from the principal and were going to book the gym space for sometime in the spring. I was shocked, to say the least, and without a moment's notice, we were on our way to doing something that I had dreamed about for years—holding a schoolwide Funball tournament. The club stated that it would use the money that it raised to benefit the March of Dimes. There was a lot of work to do, but these kids were organized, determined, and most of all passionate about Funball, and they wanted to see a successful tournament go off without a hitch.

The spring semester arrived, and I was still working with the ninth-grade students and the seniors. As the spring semester moved along, I took any opportunity that I could get to play Funball, flag tag, the blob, and capture the pig—all the games that made the day more exciting for me and the kids. I was having more fun than ever, and slowly, I started to hear the word *Funball* throughout the high school, in the cafeteria, and in the hallways. Whenever the kids had a free period and I wasn't teaching class, they would come down to the gym, and we would start pick-up games if a gym was available. These pick-up games started with about ten to fifteen kids, and within a month, about thirty to forty kids were coming down during their free periods just to play Funball.

There was still this undercurrent among some of the administrators who found Funball totally inappropriate for the high school kids. But I kept plugging along with my classes and the pick-up games.

The next thing that happened totally blew me away. While I was teaching my regular classes, kids who had free periods roamed the gym halls, looking to see what game I was playing for the day. If they looked into the gym and saw me playing floor hockey or paddleball with the kids, they would wave and walk on by. If they saw me playing Funball, they would open up the door and ask if they could play with my class. I didn't know what to think at the time. I just knew that there were kids coming down to the gym looking to play Funball even if it meant joining a class of students they didn't know. At this point, most of my classes had about twenty-two or twenty-three kids on the roster. The maximum roster size allowed was twenty-eight. So I figured if I had open spots on my roster on any given day and a student wanted to *guest play*, as I called it, how could it hurt? It was totally insane. Kids showed up at my gym class hoping that someone was absent so that they could guest play with the class. Once I created guest play, all my ninth-grade classes had twenty-eight students from that time forward.

The year was winding down, and we would soon know the number of students who had chosen specific electives for the following year. Each week, the club would stop in and give me the updates on the number of teams that had signed up for the schoolwide Funball tournament, and by tournament time, over forty-five teams of six players each had signed up for the tournament. That meant over 270 kids had signed up to come to the gym on a Friday afternoon to play in a single-elimination Funball tournament. About a week later, we got the final numbers on our elective classes, and over 220 kids had signed up for my Games class. The next day, the elder gym teacher in the department told me that 220 kids was the most who had ever signed up for any elective in the school's history. My hunch was right on the mark. These kids needed more fun—and less stress. And the numbers were the proof in the pudding.

The next stage of evolution to take place affected the entire gym department. For the past number of years, I had listened to WABC radio during my ride to and from work. In the morning, there was a show called *Curtis and Kuby*. Curtis was an ultraconservative while Kuby was as far left as you could get, and at times, he considered himself a communist. At times, I could feel my blood pressure spike when Kuby spoke on the issues of the day. It was a wonderful show, and as a result, I also started watching the Fox News channel. I would agree more often than not with the commentators, and they would always report a view other than that of the mainstream media, like ABC, CBS, and NBC. It gave me a way to stay balanced.

One Friday at the high school, I declared that all future Fridays would be known as *Fox Funball Friday*. In fun, I told the kids that Fox was Funball's official sponsor and we would become a Fox family from that moment forward at the high school. The kids went wild. As the kids came down the gym hall toward the locker room, all I would hear was "Okay, baby, welcome to Fox Funball Friday." No matter what unit we were working on, when Friday came, we would play Funball.

One Friday, one of my freshmen came into the gym and asked me if I knew what day it was. I said, "Of course I do. It is Fox Funball Friday." He said no, it wasn't; this Friday was Fox Four-Mod Funball Friday. Our school ran on a module schedule, and each mod was fifteen minutes long. Our normal classes were three mods long, but every third class, we would have a four-mod class period, which meant that we had an extra fifteen minutes to play Funball.

The kids were creating every day, and it was fun to see how their minds worked when given the right situation to be creative. Soon, many of the teachers joined in on Fox Funball Friday. The game was now evolving at such a fast pace that it was hard to keep up with all the creations that the students and the other teachers in our department made. Then one Friday, one of my co-teachers asked what I was doing for the next class period. I responded, "Are you kidding me? It is Fox Funball Friday. I am playing Prison Funball with my ninth graders."

He said, "How about a challenge? I have a class of juniors."

My next response was "Bring it on." Without even realizing it, we had started to break down the barriers that have existed for years between the different high school grade levels.

His juniors came into the gym licking their chops, just waiting to put a thumping on my young freshmen. I could see some fear in the eyes of my freshmen. I assured them that this was exactly what we needed to become better at the game. We needed to compete against those who were stronger, faster, and wiser if we were to take our Funball to the next level. The kids laughed, and I told them that I would be right there if they needed me, but to get out there and kick some junior butt.

The game was awesome! We ended up getting thrashed, but when it was over, both classes left the gym with smiles on their faces as they headed back to their academic world. We called these competitions *challenge series*, where one gym teacher would challenge another class to a competition. I can still remember the day one of my freshman classes beat a senior class. They jumped up and down as if they had just won the World Cup in soccer. They were so proud of their accomplishment, and I let them know how proud I was of them as a family. (At the start of every semester, I tell all my classes that we will be a family for the next five months, and that I have two types of families: a biological one at home, with my wife and four children, and the classes that I work with throughout the school year.)

With all the challenge series that were going on, we had brought our school community closer together. Freshmen were now familiar with some seniors because they had competed against them in Funball. Juniors were trying to take down the seniors, and it went on and on. The pick-up games in between classes had grown to about sixty kids per game, two teams of thirty, which seemed to be the maximum that we could handle safely. Whenever we had enough freshmen for the pick-up games, we would always play *freshman versus*, which meant that the freshmen would challenge all the upperclassmen in the game. The friendly pick-up games were *awesome*.

The end of the year was upon us, and it was time for the first annual Funball tournament to take place. I think we ended up with forty-nine teams in the tournament. We pulled out the center portion of the bleachers in the gym and created two courts on either end of the main gym. Every team had an official name, and a giant poster of the brackets was placed on the wall. I said a few words to start the tournament, and the next three hours were pure amazement. Boys' teams, girls' teams, and mixed teams all entered the tournament. All the kids were there just to get together after school on a Friday afternoon to have fun and try to be the first champions of the Horace Greeley Funball Tournament. The first champions were crowned—their team name was Ball Blockin'—and then it was over. What a year.

The next year came faster than ever, and this year, the majority of classes I would teach would be my Games of Life class, with one or two freshman classes as well. The kids in the Games class created every single day. And one day in particular changed Funball forever, when one of my students came up to me before class and said, "What about a power ball?"

I said, "Go on, tell me more." Well, this power ball would have special powers. If the power ball hit someone, not only would that person be eliminated, but the opposite team would get to bring a player back into the game. I said, "That sounds amazing. Let's try it today."

The power ball was brilliant and completely invented by a student, which made it even more special to me as a teacher. At this time, I was trying as hard as I could to keep up with the kids and their ideas. If they had an idea, we tried it. Some were great and helped games evolve. Others just didn't work. I would continue to remind the kids that life is just as exciting. Some days are wonderful gifts, while other days, you wish that you had never gotten out of bed. But those horrible days in our lives make the great days just that much more special when they happen.

CHAPTER 7

Nickname

I started to do something with my high school students that I had done for years as a Division I soccer coach. Each season that brought new freshmen to the program gave me opportunities to nickname those new players. I loved giving nicknames to the players; not all the players had a nickname, because they were special and you cannot just force a nickname onto a human. Nicknames had to follow the same path of evolution—they had to come naturally. If one of my college players hated his nickname, we knew it was gonna stick forever. At the high school, there were endless students, all with their special talents, quirks, nationalities, real names, and situations. My grandfather always told me to never take myself too seriously, for when you do, that is when you get yourself into trouble or get offended.

Talking with my grandfather and grandmother was always so easy and fun. Whenever they would refer to their neighbors, they always made reference to their nationalities. For example, one day, a neighbor's dogs barked all day long, and Grandpa said, "If that Russian on the corner doesn't shut those dogs up, I am gonna have to get my shotgun." And whenever he referred to the Italians on the hill, it was always, "I was up on the hill talking to the *Eye-talions* the other day." I can still remember one day my wife, Jennifer, and I took a trip up to the farm to surprise Gram and Gramps, as we called them, and as we were sitting on the porch talking about life, we started talking about how Jennifer's time in law school was going.

Grandpa said, "That's great that you are doing so good, but remember when you get done with school, you just get yourself involved with some of the Jewish folks down there in the city, and they will take good care of you." My grandpa grew up in the Czech area of Greenwich Village. Both my grandparents were Czechoslovakian and spoke the language very well. They never took the time to teach us any of the language because they believed that it was not important. What was important was to understand and master English. I only ever heard them speak Czech when they argued and they didn't want me to understand what they were saying. Even though my grandparents were Czech, my grandpa would refer to himself as a Polack whenever he told a story about screwing up in life. Not a day goes by that I don't long for those days on the porch with my grandpa, not just to be with him and listen to his wisdom but to be around that generation of people who celebrated their differences. People who never got offended when someone called them by their nationality. The reason their generation rarely got offended was because deep down inside, they knew exactly who they were. They were Americans, and Americans only. They had just come from different places around the world.

Today is different, but it doesn't stop me from searching for those special kids and people who can still have fun and enjoy a nickname for what it is. A nickname is a term of endearment. It is a sign of love. And I have had a blast over the past couple of years. My school has so many Funball players I have nicknamed that I can barely keep track of them all. Some of these kids play in the gym till their arms are about to fall off, but that doesn't stop them.

The hardest-throwing player in the school would have to be Brezhnev; he is always there with the Frominator and Rosen Rosen— all great players who will graduate this spring. J-bone lives in my office whenever he doesn't have class and is always working on his throwing techniques by himself or with the Russian. J-bone and Yormitron might be a couple of the toughest players I have ever seen take a head shot during an extreme pick-up. J-bone took a shot that popped out one of his lenses upon impact; he scrambled to pick up the pieces and remained in the game. Yormitron took an unintentional head shot with an extreme ball during a game. I immediately asked him to step off the court. After looking at him closely, I told him that he was done for the day and, if the eye continued to tear after school, to get it looked at by a doctor. He came back to gym class the next day to give me the news, smiling the entire time. He said that the eye doctor could see the imprint of the Funball through the microscope. I proclaimed that day that Yormitron would go down in history as one of the toughest players I had ever been associated with.

In all honesty, I have never had a student get a serious injury while playing Funball over the eighteen years that I have taught. Any of the injuries that I have been associated with, such as sprained ankles or pulled muscles, have happened during chasing and fleeing games that involve capturing objects—like capture the chicken or capture the pig. All the major injuries that have occurred during my career have happened while coaching at the university level, mostly knee, ankle, and shoulder injuries with a couple of broken bones as well. That's why I get so upset when I hear many parents using the angle that dodgeball is so dangerous for kids when, in reality, Funball may be one of the safest childhood games ever created.

Neanderthal tries to sneak into my gym classes almost every day, and when he plays Funball, he plays with bare feet until December rolls around. He has the highest crow-hop throw I have ever seen. One semester, I had a student whom I thought was named Hunter. He was one of the most intense, acrobatic players I had ever seen. The only problem was his real name was Harper, but I had put his name in my gradebook as Hunter. He never once corrected me during the first two months of class. One day, Graves said, "Herodes, his name is Harper." I felt so bad I had been calling him another name, and when I found out, I immediately declared that because he was such a savage player, he would be known as Hunter from that day forward. Jeffy was also in that class, and let me tell you, if Jeffy hit you with his sidearm-style throw, make no mistake, you knew you were out.

The three top-rated girls in the school, the Widow Maker, Lizard, and Raquel Raquel, can take out any boy at any time during any game. Cheryl isn't too far behind, and if you put a ball up in her catch zone, you had better start walking for the blue line, because you will be out. Nina has more heart and spirit than I have ever seen in a young lady, and she will often come down and get involved with the extreme pick-up games throughout the day.

The freshman class has a ton of spirit, and they never give, and these two character traits will assure many future victories. The Transformer, Domo, and Baby Back are a few of the freshman students who never miss a pick-up.

This year's sophomore class has a group of about forty kids who religiously come down to the gym during pick-ups. Tempelten, Spanish, the Dancing Bear, Mosca, Prime Time, Greene, Otto, Diorio, High Ball, Cookie Cutter, Petrillo, and Klein all are quality players. One sophomore in particular turned in a spectacular game: Mr. Tachanoshi scored five power goals in one game, a record that still stands today. Then there's Newman, who loves the game. He also drives me nuts sometimes, but I love the kid.

This year, some more great Funball players will be graduating: Harry, Coach, McCarthy, and Spiderman. And this year, the remaining originals will also leave our school: Sarah, Saki, Alicia, T-Bone, and Ross. These kids were involved with my very first pilot class of Games. One truly special person, who, in my mind, is a legend, will graduate this June and goes by the name of Judson. He will be dearly missed. I am proud to say that one of my former great Funballers is currently at Manhattan College working on his gym degree and vows to help promote Funball across our great country. When Kitson graduates from college, some lucky public school is going to get an amazing gym teacher. So many more wonderful players in my school all deserve to be recognized—but I would have to name all my students to do so.

Please remember I have times when I have to do things that I don't like doing to certain players when they step out of line. But as I mentioned earlier in the book, if you don't have the courage to stand up and do what is right, you have no business teaching in our public schools, so don't even bother trying to teach Funball. I absolutely hate having to send a student out of class. But the students know the rules, and the rules are for everyone. Sometimes, a one-day suspension is enough to straighten a student out. Other students need a full week to cool off before they step back into the arena. Whatever it takes to keep the gym safe, and maintain honor before, during, and after the game, I will enforce.

The year after the first Funball tournament moved along, and the second annual Funball tournament started to shape up. By tournament time, we had sixty-seven teams signed up for the tournament. I was able to get Channel 12 News to come down and do a piece on the tournament for the kids. This year's tournament was even more exciting than last year's because we had two teacher teams entered. The tournament again turned out to be a great success with lots of great victories—and many painful defeats. Just like life.

The next year's numbers had also just come in, and there were 335 students signed up to take my Games class the following year. I need to point out the fact that some students select their elective classes because they are the only classes that fit into their schedule. This is not uncommon. And even though I usually have twenty-eight students in each of my Games classes, there are still a percentage of students who would never take another gym class in their lives if they were not forced into doing so.

I hope that I have been able to paint a small picture of what life has been like for me and my students for the past three years. And I only hope that I continue to have the opportunity to teach the many different childhood games and, of course, Funball for many years to come.

CHAPTER 8

504

The 504 plan was part of the Rehabilitation Act of 1973, among other items it allows the student extended time on tests and quizzes along with other projects that are completed by the student. Dodgeball has already disappeared for many of our public schools across the country. This is a hard, cold, indisputable fact. As we all know with extinction, when it's gone, it's gone. We do not have the science yet to bring back the dinosaurs, although many are working hard on it every day. I am going to move on with my life and try not to live in the past. I need to realize that I will never change the opinions of those who hated dodgeball, nor is it my right to attempt to change their opinions. I will not cry or jump up and down, stomping my feet as I go.

As I mentioned before, all that I can do now is create an environment where kids and adults alike can come to a common ground and see things more clearly. I am going to have to work harder, dig my heels in deeper, and fight as if my life depends on the outcome to try to educate as many of my colleagues and fellow Americans about Funball, the most exciting game that has evolved over the past fifteen years, and to also bring them up to date with what is happening every day in our public schools. As I mentioned before, our public schools are under assault. This assault has already taken down dodgeball, and many more of the traditions that made our school system one of the best in the world.

Honestly, at this point in time, my opinion is that our public schools are not even in the top 10 percent among those in nations around the world. And I now understand the true nature of why our public schools are failing, and it is very simple. We cater to the minority rather than the majority.

You have all heard the saying, "The squeaky wheel gets the grease." Many believe that saying to be strictly American, but that is not the case at all. China has a similar saying but with a completely different emphasis placed on the outcome. They say, "The bird whose head sticks out gets shot." In American public schools, the parent or community member who screams the loudest is always coddled, massaged, placated, and catered to. Let me emphasize again that the overwhelming majority of parents in our public schools are wonderful, supportive, creative participants in their children's education. Only a small part of the population yells and tries to change the policies that will ultimately affect all public school children across our country. And this total desire to please everyone, all the time, has led us down this road of mediocrity. Once these parents feel that their issues have been dealt with to their liking, they fade away for a while until they are unhappy again. This is exactly how dodgeball met its untimely death, along with many other great traditions that produced so many great students throughout the years.

Now, I realize that China is still largely communist, and we just can't shoot those people in our communities who are always bellyaching. But we can educate those parents and people, and while educating them, take our time when we make decisions on changes that will ultimately affect our students into the future. If we continue to water down our curriculum and cave to every public interest group, we stand no chance of surviving into the future. Many people believe that our public schools need a complete overhaul. That is not the case—yet. We may have one more chance before a total reconstruction needs to take place. What our public schools need are more teachers and administrators with the *courage*, *wisdom*, and *conviction* to discipline today's students, and do what is right for our kids no matter what 2 percent of the community's population thinks. If some parents continue to make excuses for their children's weaknesses, we don't stand a chance.

If your child is weak in a specific academic area, he or she gets extra help or tutoring. Tutoring has become one of the biggest industries in our country. Well, if your child has a social weakness, or a weakness with fears, anger, or jealousy, you parents need to force him or her to get involved with those situations that create those uncomfortable feelings. This is the only way that these children will ever overcome those emotions that cause them so much suffering. More and more students are being falsely labeled with various disabilities and handicaps. As a result, a very large percentage of students receive extended time on their exams and other projects that are due throughout the school year.

What world do you know of that functions on extended time as a matter of survival and evolution? I could just see the caveman after his spear flies past the tiger's head, missing it completely. The caveman quickly holds up his 504 Plan that is etched on a piece of slate as the tiger bears down on him in the forest. The tiger stops, looks at the document, and signals that it is authentic. The tiger mentions that one day, the Cats and Reptile Foundation will get enough resources to overturn that disabilities act that has been in place for the past two thousand years. "But until then, I will abide by the tribal council's decision. OK, I will go back into the woods and hide again. You will receive your second chance to kill me as it is written in your 504 Plan, but if you miss this time, it will be dinnertime for my little cubs."

Natural evolution had that particular caveman ripped to shreds, and as a result, his genetic clan would soon die off due to his horrible aim with a spear and inability to run fast enough after the tiger had his turn. When the tiger next encountered a totally different caveman who was stronger and faster, and had better aim, the caveman killed the tiger and then gained the right to reproduce and pass on that stronger, faster, smarter clan of cavemen.

When I took a test years ago as a high school or college student, when the test time was over, I handed in the test. If I couldn't finish the test and, as a result, I didn't gain enough points to pass the test, I failed the test. End of story. If it became a pattern, then I would be forced to switch to a different level of class, one that I might have a chance to succeed in. Or, in this situation, a student would veer off on an entirely different path that perhaps was not based in the academic realm. I understand what these children's parents are trying to do. They want the same opportunities for their children as every other child gets in our public schools. My question to those parents is this: Is that philosophy based in reality? Does every human possess the same exact abilities? The answer is no.

I predict that it is only a matter of time before the 504 Plans are incorporated into high school and college sports. This is what it would look like. Here we are at the New York State Class AA football title game at the Carrier Dome on the Syracuse University campus. We have the high-scoring Panthers taking on the Badgers with their impressive time-of-possession percentage. What a game it has been, and we find the teams tied with six seconds on the clock and the Badgers setting up for what seems to be a thirty-two-yard field goal attempt to win the state title.

Joey Chittenfield, the Badgers kicker, is walking out onto the field to get ready for the attempt. *Joey 504*, as his teammates affectionately call him due to his 504 Plan that he has had for the past two seasons, signals to the referees and holds up his right wrist, which has the yellow 504 wristband attached firmly to it. The referee signals up to the control booth with his two hands separating during the signal. Then, the new state-of-the-art goalposts start to widen the extra twenty feet that is allowed to all 504 kickers in the state association. Here's the snap, the hold. The kick is up, it's on its way, it has the distance, it is starting to hook to the right, it hits the inside of the goalpost and goes through. The Badgers have just won the 2015 New York State AA football championship on Joey Chittenfield's thirty-two-yard field goal. The crowd of spectators rush the field as they carry Joey off on their shoulders.

Now, that may sound ridiculous, and it might be. But I am sure that some attorney will attempt to create that very situation within the next ten years in our public schools if something isn't done to stop the madness.

So now that student heads out into the real world and soon realizes that a capitalistic society cannot function with that format. You will never see the CEO of General Electric making a phone call to the CEO of Sony over in Japan, asking them to give General Electric some extended time to flesh out their chip technology before Sony unveils their product. The world that we live in is very competitive and filled with pressure at every turn. If we can't produce students who have the ability to thrive and create in this environment, other countries will. In the past thirty or forty years, the global economy has driven the speed of evolution, and the truth is that many of our students cannot keep pace with the world. We have been the greatest country on this planet and still maintain the most powerful influence over the other nations of the world. But as each year passes by and we continue to produce subpar students for the work force, we will continue to lose ground to the other nations around the world. Some factors are out of our control, but one is very much in our control, and it is our education system.

Let's return to the 504 Plan. Most children who receive these plans don't want them. They themselves have told me that they don't like having the extra time for tests and projects but that their parents have convinced them that they need them to keep pace with the rest of the students around them. The adults are, of course, the driving force behind these many different accommodations that certain students receive. Please try to understand that I am aware that school districts need special education programs. They have been around for years. When the amount of students who receive extended time reaches 30 to 40 percent of the entire population of a particular school, it spells disaster for the future.

I am well aware that as I give my opinion on the issues that have killed dodgeball, many of my colleagues will take offense and have huge issues with what I have written. But really, dodgeball is just the tip of the iceberg, and what will come next is our great country's inability to lead the world both socially and economically. The fact is that not everyone can be a doctor or an engineer. No one in our public schools has the courage to actually say what I just put down on paper. But it is the truth. And if we are to survive, we have to stop ignoring the truth and start developing options for our students who may not have the same intellectual abilities as others in our culture. I told you at the beginning of the book that I am not an intellectual person, and if you put me in a room filled with scholars to discuss technological advances in the computer-chip world, I would be like a fish out of water. But if you put me in that same room with those same scholars and the discussion centered on the ability to see everyday situations clearly, or how to bring people together to work toward a common goal, I would be fine.

I was just speaking with my sister-in-law, who teaches in another school district in Westchester County, New York. I happened to ask her what percentage of her kids receive extended time in the third grade. *Thirty-four percent* of the third-grade students receive extended time for testing! That means thirty-four students out of one hundred receiving extended time for exams. I think that many of our public schools have done a very good job of hiding the facts for the past twenty years, and if our American industries truly understood what we are doing with our students, they would spend more time getting involved with our education system.

I don't mean to indict the entire public school system here. But if administrators continue to allow these parents to come in and demand that their son or daughter receive a 504 Plan for extended time, we don't stand a chance of surviving into the future, let alone evolving as a society. So don't send in a note excusing your child because he or she doesn't feel well on the day that he or she has to give a speech in front of the class. I know that your child is scared to death of getting up in front of the class and speaking, but that is exactly what he or she needs to do to overcome those fears. Always remember you may have helped your child get through that speech class in high school. But what is going to happen six years from now, when he or she has to give the presentation before the board of directors for the new energy proposal?

CHAPTER 9

A Second Chance

Parents also have to master the very important ability to know when to let go and allow their child to fail or succeed. This is not as easy as just making excuses for your child. This means having the wisdom to clearly recognize when to allow your child the space and opportunity to be mindful of his or her own progress as it relates to school and day-to-day existence. It is a wonder so many other generations survived largely on their own, creating every day. Some of us are forced to let our kids move on even after a very traumatic situation occurs when they are small children. For some, it may take many years to hand over the reins.

My wife and I are among those who have had to become mindful of this philosophy every day. We have had to allow our second child to venture off on his own even after we almost lost him when he was only five years old. I have decided to tell this story for two reasons: (1) to help me continue to evolve on my path as I strive to survive the greatest challenge I have ever undertaken, called *parenthood*, and (2) to perhaps help another parent realize that our children's lives are all that matter, and once we decide to have a child, we will be his or her parent until we pass away.

This incident took place at a soccer and pool party at the end of June 2001. Normally, my wife would always take the kids to these types of parties, but for some reason, I agreed to go to this one. Some religions call it *fate*; some *destiny*. I don't have an answer for why I was there that day, but I decided to go with my wife and kids. When we arrived at the pool, I was holding the baby while my wife was putting sunscreen on our third child, Avery. Anton, the oldest, was already jumping and diving into the deep end, while Aiden, five years old, was in the shallow end. Within what seemed like seconds, Anton called over to me to tell me that Aiden was in the pool. I responded by saying I already knew he was in the shallow end. Anton replied that Aiden was over there on the bottom of the pool under the diving board.

I was sitting only three feet from the edge of the pool. I don't recall what I did with my baby, Holden, but in the next second, I was sky-diving into the pool, scanning the bottom of the pool while I was still in the air, and what I saw horrified me. I clearly saw the distinctive blue-and-orange swim trunks on the bottom of the pool. Those swim trunks were Aiden's. He was lying stretched out on his back when I reached him.

As I lifted him onto the concrete and laid him on his back, I saw only signs that were not what you wanted to see from a child who was under the water for any amount of time. He was lifeless, catatonic, blue, and, most horrific of all, not breathing. I immediately went into rescue breathing, and after the first set, I rolled him over on his side as water and vomit started to gush out of his mouth. I paused for a second to quickly look for any signs of life. Nothing, so I went into the second set of breaths, again rolling him over to allow the water and vomit to exit his body. And as I continued, I couldn't help but realize that Aiden was no longer a boy; he was a body. A boy could laugh, cry, and show emotion. A body could do none of that, and that was exactly what he was at this time. Again, no signs of breathing or movement, so I went into the third set of rescue breaths. The same pattern continued with water and vomit exiting the body, but no signs of life whatsoever.

After the third set of rescue breaths, I must admit that all my years of training as a first responder and all the statistics that I was well aware of flashed through my mind. Usually after the third set of rescue breaths, if there were no signs of life, the chances of survival went down drastically. So in the very same thought, I said to myself that I could not believe that I was losing a child today—that my five-year-old son was being taken away from me at such a young age. He had just learned how to ride his bike with the training wheels off the week before. Only five years of life on this earth; that's not how it was supposed to happen. Your kids were supposed to grow up, grow old, and outlive you.

As those thoughts raced through my mind, I was already into the fourth set of rescue breaths. After this set of rescue breaths, I just couldn't put Aiden back onto the hard, cold, damp concrete. I took his little body and brought it close to mine, gently holding him on his side with his face near my chest as the life drained out of my son. I had never felt such sorrow in my life. His skin was turning darker shades of blue by the second. Every second seemed like an hour. Time had stopped, almost as if to make sure that I was being punished for my lack of attentiveness, lack of responsibility, lack of everything that you were supposed to have as a good parent. Time had stopped to make sure that I felt the full effect of the pain that I was meant to endure. As my son lay lifeless in my arms, I was still very aware of my surroundings, because I remember my son Anton asking me, "Hey, Dad, how is Aiden doing?"

And I responded, "He is not doing too good right now. He needs some help."

And seconds after I responded to Anton, I felt a very slight twinge in Aiden's right arm. Then a muscle moved in his right leg. I quickly lowered him onto his back with my arms still under his head and waist. Then a very quick spasm came from his back. Moments later, both eyes opened up, and his face took on a look of fear that I had never seen before. Still five or six seconds passed before he finally took his first breath. It was a long, wheezy, labored breath that immediately started to fade his skin's horrific shade of blue. Another deep breath, and then, he started screaming as if he had seen a ghost. I quickly lifted him back up into my arms and started walking down the street toward the ambulance that was on its way.

We raced toward the local hospital only to find that it was not equipped to handle pediatric drowning victims. So Aiden and I were then airlifted to the regional medical center. Aiden just lay there on the stretcher hooked up to all the tubes. He stared straight up at the inside of the helicopter. He would not communicate with any of the emergency personnel. Every moment that passed by gave my mind time to travel to the most distant, painful consequences possible.

Once we touched down and they raced him into the trauma center, I let go of his hand, and for the first time since I had lifted Aiden from the bottom of the pool, we were separated. During that separation, I realized that I might have lost my son, the son I had grown to know over five years. He was clearly going to survive, but at what cost? A lonely, cold, hollow feeling stayed with me while I sat down in the hallway, leaning against the wall.

My wife had not yet arrived at the hospital. After about one hour, the neurologists came out with big smiles on their faces to give me the good news that his brain was fine but that his lungs had a large amount of water still present and they would have to keep him for the next couple of days. I just sat in the hallway, leaning against the wall with my head down, trying to understand all that had just taken place.

It wouldn't be until the next day that Aiden would finally speak with me. His first words were those of a question. His eyebrows turned down as he asked me, "Dad, where were you? I was waiting at the bottom of the pool for you to pick me up, but you never came."

Realizing that he had lain there on his back at the bottom of the pool, still conscious, was almost too much to bear. I said, "I am sorry, Aiden, but I got there as quick as I could."

He said, "It's OK." And this is the part of the story that I hope many will try to understand: that my wife and I had to stay very mindful not to coddle and treat Aiden differently than any other normal five-year-old boy. We still had to allow him to go into water, go places with his young friends in the backyard. We had been given a second chance with our second son, and we wanted to make the most of that chance. But in doing so, we also had to realize that he needed to feel all the physical pain that a young boy must feel from wounds and all the emotional pain from competing while playing games with other young kids. We had to treat him just like any of our other three children. And this is the message that I hope all parents will understand as they help guide their children through life. And always do what you feel is best for your child, but don't force your beliefs onto mine. This belief will help our public schools survive into the future. We will raise our children in many different ways, forms, beliefs, religions, traditions, and so on, and that is what makes life in America so great.

Before I end, I would like to tie in one more example of how some of my generation of American parents send many mixed messages to their children, and as a result try to send those same messages to my children by attempting to completely eliminate dodgeball. And please remember, this is just my opinion, and you must do what you believe is best for your child and your family. I am not judging you on how you decide to handle the situation, so please extend me the same courtesy.

Again, parents send these mixed messages with the best of intentions. But as I have already pointed out, we, as parents, need to have not only good intentions but the ability to look at how those intentions and decisions will affect our kids today, tomorrow, and into the future. It is almost as if some of my generation of parents truly believe that they are the first generation to raise human infants. And they will accept no one's opinion when it comes to doing what is best for their child, which is fine, because that is their right as a parent in America—at least for now it is.

I watched a recent *20/20, Dateline,* or other evening news program piece on three generations living in the same household, mainly due to marital or financial situations with the young family. This evening news story was all about how the two generations were clashing when it came to disciplining the little ones in the house. Grandma and Grandpa were not shy when they talked about what had worked for them years ago, and the new parents, or younger-generation parents, wanted something better for their children when it came to discipline. Grandma sternly said, "I believe in smacking the little ones on the hands when they do something wrong." Having had the opportunity to know my grandparents on my father's side for over thirty years, I am *well aware* of how my parents' generation was raised, by the many stories my grandfather and grandmother told. Most of those stories involved handing out discipline with a primitive weapon of sorts.

Then Mom's turn came to enlighten the world on how Grandma was sending mixed messages by smacking the child on the hand, especially after the child had just smacked someone else. The mom said that Grandma was confusing her two-year-old when it came to the child hitting another child or adult. She asked how one could smack the child on the back of the hand and in the same breath say, "We don't hit."

Here, some of our new generation of parents see things differently than our parents or grandparents. This is where the younger parents don't see the true nature of the situation, or they just don't understand the human being. Three things motivate a two-year-old: (1) hunger, (2) fear, and (3) pain. Two-year-olds don't yet have the ability to understand logic, unlike many of their parents would have you believe. So you want something better for your child than what you had when you were a kid? Well, I have the answer: Funball. Your kid needs more Funball.

When your two-year-old starts to walk out into the street in front of your house, right in front of a fully loaded oil truck, are you going to take your little child by the hand, slowly take her out of the street, and sit her down to discuss physics, talking about how it would be very bad if the force of the truck plus the truck's mass hit the child? "You see, honey, you only weigh about eighteen pounds; the truck weighs about twelve thousand. You are walking about five-tenths a mile per hour, and the truck is traveling about forty-five miles per hour. If you were to be hit by that big oil truck, you would get a big boo-boo, and we don't want that, now, do we? So do you understand?"

You may have just saved your little child that moment on that day, and while doing so made yourself feel better by taking the time to sit down and talk to your child about what is right and what is wrong. But what about two weeks from then, when you are on the phone with a very important business client and something is going wrong with the account and you take your eye off your child for just one moment? I just shared a story with you where my wife and I took our eyes off one of our kids for a split second. Do you really feel confident that your two-year-old won't walk into the street again because of the long, heartfelt discussion that you had two weeks ago? Or is there a little doubt in the back of your mind?

Now, let's rewind. Let's go back two weeks, when your child was running into the street in front of the oil truck. This time, you grab her by the hand, pull her back into the front yard, and give her a smack on the tail end that stings like a bee. Then you raise your voice, point to the street, and say, "No!" three times in a row. Then you give her one more sting on the tail for good measure. Two completely different ways of handling the situation, but both of which you have the right to carry out as a parent in America.

Let me remind you that some states are pushing for a ban on spanking your own child. As I mentioned before, however you feel fit to raise your child is right for you, and I won't condemn you for using the time-out chair if you will mind your own business when it comes to my children and my discipline style. This is the belief structure that has single-handedly eliminated dodgeball for so many young children across our great country, and it must stop now, or else many more great opportunities will be lost forever.

Remember, three of the greatest motivators for us as humans are fear, pain, and hunger. The second scenario covered two of the three motivating factors that affect us as humans. It scared the little one to death when Mommy grabbed her by the arm and screamed no. Then the little one felt pain as a result of walking onto that flat, black, hot area in front of the house. Our little ones may not be able to utilize logic until they are older, but their memory is working and growing from the day they take their first breath. They remember that if they cry while in their crib, they will get picked up. So the next time your two-year-old heads toward the flat, black, hot area in front of the house, keep in mind that he will never remember that it is called a *street*, or that a truck weighs more than he does, or that the big truck might give him a boo-boo. He will remember that he got spanked on his butt when he walked on the black area, and that it hurt when his mom or dad smacked his butt. "I don't want to feel that sting again, so maybe I will stay on this green area that is soft and doesn't hurt when I fall."

You may not have wanted to do that to your child the day she walked out in front of that oil truck, but remember we have the responsibility to do what is right for our kids today, tomorrow, and into the future.

In spite of what you may think, you cannot be with your child every moment of every day, just as you can't be with your kid when he or she is in gym class or on the playground. So please continue to do what you believe is right for your child. But when it comes to mine or thousands of other children across the country, try to see the true nature of Funball. Try to see how it has followed the natural path of evolution and why so many kids today need this game and many other games like it to survive in this modern world. Allow me—and many other gym teachers across the country—to keep your children young for as long as we can by playing the many games that made us who we are today.

We must realize that dodgeball was life, and now, dodgeball may be gone. But Funball will give your children the ability to see the true nature of life and, as a result, will help them with the endless struggles that they will encounter for many years to come. For those kids who are born with the seed of anger, if Funball is taught correctly, it will teach them patience and humility, and that losing doesn't cost us the deed to our house. And for those children who are born with the seed of fear, Funball can give them that confidence to realize that getting hit in the stomach with a ball isn't going to put them in the hospital or kill them.

I have always had a problem with the old saying "That which doesn't kill us only makes us stronger." That's a catchy saying, but it is not based in truth. The phrase needs to state, "That which doesn't kill us only makes us wiser." You never gain any strength by falling twenty feet to the ground while climbing the tree in your backyard. Those broken ribs and that punctured lung will not make you a stronger human. But they will make you wiser, because you won't step on an old dead branch next time you climb a tree.

I think that we would all agree that our kids will face many challenges that people didn't even think about when we were kids. And we would like to think that we have become more civilized. It is a fact that we have become more civilized, but that doesn't mean that we have stopped evolving. We will continue to evolve until circumstances bring our evolution to an end, be it a catastrophic environmental encounter with an asteroid, disease, nuclear war, or our sun burning out. And even if the human race were to become extinct, certain life forms would continue on and evolve into the infinite future. We cannot concern ourselves with the many ways that could end civilization. The mainstream media perpetuates most of these situations to scare the population into submission. What we can control are our day-to-day lives as we continue to raise our children, create our traditions, and do what we believe to be right as Americans.

So if you truly believe that it is in your child's best interest to not play Funball, send in a note, and I will let him or her ride the stationary bike in the fitness center. But please don't make a run for the next board of education election so that you can ban the game for the many thousands of children who need and love the game. Remember, we are humans, and as humans, we are subject to certain truths. We are born, we are children, we become adults, we age, and then one day, we will die. No one can dispute these truths. My career has focused on the truth that we are all children during this lifetime, and when we are kids, we love and need to play games. Every child will have all the time in the world to be an adult and to struggle with the many ups and downs that life will throw at him or her. Help me help your child stay young for as long as he or she can. If dreams and memories sometimes get confused, that's as it should be. Every kid deserves to be a hero; every kid already is a hero. Those are the wonder years.

I would like to end with one of the greatest lines about life that I have ever heard. Remember, this is one gym teacher's opinion. Norm Peterson said it best when he walked into Cheers one evening. Sammy asked him, "How is it going, Norm?"

Norm replied, "Sammy, it's a dog-eat-dog world out there, and I am wearing Milk-Bone underwear."